Aromatherapy

A Symphony of Colored Energy and Aromatic Scents

(How to Use Essential Oils to Improve Health and Well-being at Home)

Arthur Orlowski

Published By **Phil Dawson**

Arthur Orlowski

Aromatherapy: A Symphony of Colored Energy and Aromatic Scents (How to Use Essential Oils to Improve Health and Well-being at Home)

ISBN   978-1-7780570-6-9

No part of this guidebook shall be reproduced in any form without permission in writing from the publisher except in the case of brief quotations embodied in critical articles or reviews.

Legal & Disclaimer

The information contained in this book is not designed to replace or take the place of any form of medicine or professional medical advice. The information in this book has been provided for educational & entertainment purposes only.

The information contained in this book has been compiled from sources deemed reliable, and it is accurate to the best of the Author's knowledge; however, the Author cannot guarantee its accuracy and validity and cannot be held liable for any errors or omissions. Changes are periodically made to this book. You must consult your doctor or get professional medical advice before using any of the suggested remedies, techniques, or information in this book.

Table Of Contents

Chapter 1: Aroma What? 1

Chapter 2: The Information...................... 4

Chapter 3: Is Aromatherapy Effective? 7

Chapter 4: How To Use Aromatherapy At Domestic... 11

Chapter 5: Affecting The Limbic System. 15

Chapter 6: Utilizing Essential Oils........... 18

Chapter 7: How To Use Thoroughly 38

Chapter 8: Carrier Oils........................... 43

Chapter 9: Other Resources About Absolutes 48

Chapter 10: Promoting Emotional Well-Being With Aromatherapy 54

Chapter 11: Is Aromatherapy Effective For Weight Loss?... 63

Chapter 12: Essential Oil Blending 65

Chapter 13: The Use Of Diffusers........... 72

Chapter 14: Storing Essential Oils 76

Chapter 15: The Skinny On Essential Oils 79

Chapter 16: Choosing And Using High-Quality Essential Oils............................ 109

Chapter 17: Best Essential Oils For Anxiety 134

Chapter 18: Best Essential Oils For Happiness 159

Chapter 19: Best Essential Oils For Memory And Concentration 177

Chapter 1: Aroma What?

It's possible that you are familiar with aromatherapy and as a minimum recognize a touch bit approximately what it carries. You recognise how aromatherapy uses scents and odors to treat illnesses and problems? However, that does appear a touch first rate. Just via smelling a few element, how is it even viable?

Do now not be involved; you aren't the handiest one which has doubts. Others have regularly confused the efficacy of this remedy technique. What precisely is the intended direction of movement? To apprehend how aromatherapy works, if it sincerely works in any respect, we want to have a higher information of what it without a doubt is.

Actually, the term "aromatherapy" is a significant one which encompasses lots of styles of traditions that use plant material and critical oils to enhance someone's pleasant of existence on the identical time as furthermore fostering a more high-quality surroundings. Aromatherapy, in area of "actual" medical treatments, is the term used to explain all present day treatments used during the Western civilized worldwide that appoint vital oils and plant recall. Aromatherapy is a sort of remedy typically used to resource in rest or stress discount. Essential oils and volatile plant oils are used in aromatherapy to offer emotional and physical effects. It is used as a form of complementary treatment to decorate someone's fitness or temper and commonly consists of fragrant compounds made from risky plant substances, important oils, or similar natural devices.

Due to all of these numerous packages, aromatherapy is a completely properly-favored possibility remedy technique. Many people have decided on to rent aromatherapy to assist them acquire the favored us of a of being due to the fact they dislike the every so often unpleasant facet outcomes of prescribed remedy, particularly for depression, stress, or other comparable conditions. When used nicely or with a doctor's approval, aromatherapy has been shown to be useful in some conditions. You can also moreover bear in mind some of the ones humans as oddballs for choosing it over particular synthetic capsules.

Chapter 2: The Information

Since historical times, aromatherapy has been implemented in a few ability. In an try to address illnesses and remedy illnesses, humans have hired plant fabric and important oils for masses of years. Because of this, it is hard to pinpoint the transport and improvement of aromatherapy with a selected date or timeline of activities. Due to the evolving goals of many cultures, it has developed through the years to healthful the ones wishes specifically. With the invention and use of latest plant fabric and vital oils, it has additionally altered.

Due to this records's chronic change, vital oils were advanced using distilled plant cloth, which added about the improvement of aromatherapy in its modern shape. It is feasible to hint the improvement of this unique distillation approach decrease returned to the 20th century. Aromatherapy became first used by a French chemist named Renée Maurice Gattefosse in 1920, in step with how the term is presently utilized in medication.

Renee Maurice Gattefosse have turn out to be a well-known French chemist who devoted his existence to learning about and studying the healing blessings of crucial oils. A fortuitous occurrence in his laboratory sooner or later stimulated him to dedicate himself to this cause. In his haste to vicinity out the flames after through coincidence setting his arm on fireside, Gattefosse ran around his lab. Renée Maurice Gattefosse, a French chemist, came decided a massive open jar of lavender oil even as looking for the closest vat of liquid to paste his arm into. The chemist hurriedly dipped his arm into the lavender oil to douse the flames, but to his amazement, he felt almost immediately pain comfort. Gattefosse moreover placed that his burns recovered specifically brief and left very minor scarring due to this lifestyles-converting stumble upon. He become astounded via the difference in the healing of those wounds that have been protected in lavender oil in evaluation to the commonplace burns that the chemist had professional. The French scientist Renée Maurice Gattefosse made some of crucial discoveries, however one of the most vital have end up that lavender oil sped up healing regular and left scars and contamination to a minimal.

Renée Maurice Gattefosse changed right right into a French chemist whose studies have become simplest carried on through Jean Valnet at some point of World War II. The gangrene that troubled injured soldiers become treated by the use of Jean Valnet the use of vital oils and different distilled plant material. Using the ones crucial oils, Jean Valnet emerge as frequently able to keep infantrymen' lives, albeit it wasn't normally a treatment. This end up a extraordinarily beneficial finding all through times of army crisis.

Chapter 3: Is Aromatherapy Effective?

When most human beings undergo in mind aromatherapy, they often ask this query. Is aromatherapy a scam or does it in reality art work? Aromatherapy isn't always new, irrespective of what many humans maintain in mind. At least eighty years have exceeded seeing that the appearance of aromatherapy and its subsequent reputation. But aromatherapy has existed for hundreds of years in its number one shape.

To begin with, do no longer be duped by using way of corporations that try to pass off their fragrant gadgets as aromatherapy objects. Some companies will sell bogus aromatherapy claims as a way to boom profits. Aromatherapy is treated further to different chemical materials in international places much like the US, in which the FCC mandates correct element identity. Make sure the product you have been considering includes certainly natural factors and not one of the individual-made range. What about crucial conditions? Can aromatherapy without a doubt resource in the remedy of illnesses or highbrow problems? The reality is that strain or an sickness can't be cured via manner of the usage of aromatherapy. Anyone who seeks out aromatherapy in the hopes of finding a treatment may be allow down. Simply positioned, this isn't always how aromatherapy features.

Aromatherapy, however, is meant to reinforce your temper, momentarily lessen tension, or assist with exceptional mental ailments similarly to helping you manipulate with a physical situation or the signs of an infection. This does now not endorse that each one of those symptoms or troubles will disappear. It without a doubt approach that aromatherapy should make dealing with those symptoms and problems a good deal much less complicated. Neither most cancers nor AIDS, nor precise immoderate ailments, can be cured by the usage of aromatherapy. Instead, it may resource in calming the anxiety, easing motion illness, and enhancing one's widespread disposition. Any immoderate contamination have to not ever be dealt with with it due to the truth the mainstay of care. It truely serves as a help for precise treatment plans which may be already in area as a complimentary treatment. In some situations, it could be capable of alternative for chemical prescription or OTC medicinal tablets. For instance, it may be of massive use in treating indigestion, infection, pores and pores and skin conditions, hygiene troubles, wounds, and intellectual or emotional issues.

Additionally, every body who makes use of aromatherapy will enjoy its effects in a fantastic way. Your sensory reminiscence can also have an impact on while or how well remedy works for you. As a result, if you have a awful revel in with a advantageous experience, it won't have the preferred impact on you.

Do a few studies approximately the enterprise wherein you want to get your essential oils or different ingredients for aromatherapy remedies. Make wonderful they employ best natural substances and provide you with accurate instructions at the way to apply the aromatherapy materials. For example, be cautious of organizations that advise you to apply critical oils to your pores and pores and skin. Only diluted important oils must be carried out to the pores and skin. Numerous devices inside the market were mislabeled, and there can be a super deal of fake cloth approximately aromatherapy that can also make untrue claims approximately the purported healing advantages of aromatherapy oils.

Chapter 4: How To Use Aromatherapy At Domestic

For some situations, aromatherapy may be used as a shape of remedy or prevention. It also can be pretty effective at decreasing stress levels. The limbic gadget, specifically, the perfume middle of the mind, are extensively impacted thru the crucial oils which may be emitted in the course of aromatherapy. Numerous early clinical studies imply a synergy some of the frame's recovery techniques and aromatic oils, even though no particular clinical studies have not started established the fitness blessings of aromatherapy on the body. Due to the fact that the ones aromatic oils are regularly burned at some point of aromatherapy, they're frequently discharged as gas or vapor.

Even in case you are not privy to it, aromatherapy is used regularly for the duration of the English-talking globe. Many people in Western civilizations might not continually understand it as aromatherapy, however they frequently use perfumes, rubdown oils, and scented lotions of their each day lives. This is one motive why many practitioners want to emphasise how they use incense and rubdown oils for aromatherapy. Only within the United States and awesome English-speaking countries is aromatherapy regarded as the sort of supplemental remedy.

Have you ever worn perfume to advantage a selected perfume? Have you ever used creams that made you experience quite snug for no obvious cause? Have you ever smoked incense with names like "Tranquility," finding it to be rather calming and thrilling? Have you ever used bath cleansing cleaning soap or a few different type of bath lotion purported to assist loosen up and soothe?

All of these are complementing features of aromatherapy. These are all techniques that people hire aromas, scents, and different factors of nature to help create a relaxing, cushty, and inviting surroundings.

Aromatherapy is a part of the standard of care in France, wherein it end up first decided. The utilization of vital oils' numerous blessings, which encompass their antiseptic, antiviral, antifungal, and antibacterial developments, is tremendously valued within the route of France. They may additionally discover similar developments in precise distilled plant material and hire them to save you the spread of illnesses. Compared to the techniques used in plenty of English-speaking countries, this is rather fantastic. Essential oils which might be administered through a physician are regularly given to patients in France and its neighboring international locations.

Do you have got got any concept how that might be inside the US? Imagine consulting a scientific physician who endorsed aromatherapy as a pressure-reduction technique instead of a artificial drug. This can be very numerous from what Western societies are used to. However, aromatherapy is applied in a plethora of other international locations as a method of every contamination prevention and sickness treatment. Despite numerous enhancements made inside the concern of aromatherapy medication, the united states, Russia, Germany, or Japan have no longer authorized contemporary-day aromatherapy as a legitimate medical department. In those nations, doctors frequently fail to famend the advantages of aromatherapy treatments. However, there are nonetheless many countries inside the path of the area that use aromatherapy to address illnesses and illnesses and prevent them from spreading. Despite the clean benefits of aromatherapy in reducing stress tiers, maximum doctors in Western societies do now not need the usage of it to address stress.

Chapter 5: Affecting The Limbic System

You might also now not right now see the advantages of aromatherapy. Understanding how aromatherapy in reality competencies permit you to higher keep near how it could be of assist. Aromatherapy in stylish affects the limbic system. The clinical profession has defined the limbic machine as a set of mind areas that assist severa cognitive techniques. Both the mobility and reminiscence mind techniques are maintained by the limbic machine of the thoughts. Together with the endocrine machine and the autonomic anxious tool, this mind tool capabilities. The limbic system has the potential to have an impact on the amount of pleasure experienced thru the endocrine gadget. The same location of the mind is involved in other immoderate endorphin reviews in addition to sexual delight.

Aromatherapy can be a useful approach to employ or comply with therapy to the limbic tool of the brain because of the massive impact that a perfume ought to have in bringing approximately specific recollections or emotions.

There are many aromatherapy scents and sensations related to them; the scents are intended to deliver all over again glad reminiscences of a happy time or vicinity for the person using them. Because of this limbic tool reaction, seasonal scents are applied in masses of aromatherapy merchandise with a few diploma of fulfillment.

The cinnamon candle can regularly convey returned excursion memories or make someone feel just like Christmas. Have you ever confused why a positive experience or smell will conjure up snap shots of particular places, humans, or gadgets? Have you ever located that whilst some smells should in all likelihood make you experience comfortable and at domestic and convey decrease returned extremely good reminiscences, distinctive smells may additionally want to have the exact opposite effect? This is lots like how aromatherapy operates. The fragrances and scents will reason certain bodily reactions in you in case you need to have the popular effect.

Chapter 6: Utilizing Essential Oils

Finding the quality essential oils

The use of vital oils in aromatherapy is large. At least 15 superb issuer oils are regularly utilized in aromatherapy, collectively with at the least 90 excellent vital and pure oils. It is comprehensible that maximum people find it hard to determine which important oils can be first-rate for their personal meant impact while there are such numerous alternatives to be had. If you pick out to exercising aromatherapy, it's far important to research the numerous varieties of oils to pick the most effective that might artwork exceptional for you.

Since undiluted crucial oils are frequently of a healing grade, it's also viable to choose out them from awesome gadgets which can be comparable and proper for aromatherapy. Of course, if you stay in a rustic wherein the area is regulated, then this is simplest a beneficial benchmark to use. Oil difficulty content fabric is standardized inside the US thru using FCC labeling. FCC labeling refers back to the Food Chemical Codex, and it is a fashionable set by means of the use of the FCC that establishes the favored concentrations of a certain fragrance and generating chemical in the oil.

This form of control is hired to hold at least a minimum degree of requirements in the aromatherapy industry. The FCC now not handiest aids in regulating aromatherapy however furthermore in identifying what kinds of oils and critical plant material are maximum suitable for certain recuperation techniques. Furthermore, this guiding principle specifies how a good deal of a high-quality oil must be used for a particular function, getting rid of the concern of using an excessive amount of of all people oil. However, there can be no rule that forbids a producer from together with a artificial element to satisfy any necessities set via the FCC for any precise oil.

However, the best manner to inform if an important oil can be truely beneficial is really to use your nose. Many people who interest on aromatherapy are capable of telling if a perfume is synthetic or herbal. As prolonged as someone is willing to place in the effort and time, it is believed that during fact anyone can studies this abilities. You should make every attempt to use herbal oils and elements for aromatherapy each time possible.

It's vital to paste near your herbal preference irrespective of what treatment, feel, or perfume you turn out to be deciding on. It's in all likelihood that you can love the use of an oil if you want the manner it smells or makes you revel in. Regardless rely what the suitable oil or aroma is supposed to gain or the way it must benefit you, it will in all likelihood be useless if you do not understand the scent and revel in using it as a form of treatment. Your body is making an attempt to provide you with a warning to hold searching if you do now not similar to the aroma of a first-rate critical oil.

How to assess an oil for first-class

It is critical that you pattern efficiently while you're out trying out severa essential oil sorts to your aromatherapy. Simply pry open the bottle of oil about 3 to 4 inches underneath your nose to take a sample. Gently inhale at the same time as slowly rocking the bottle from proper to left. It's essential to keep away from taking inhalations which is probably too deep or the usage of the bottle as an inhaler. Deeper inhalation of the aroma will now not boom its effectiveness and may also be dangerous due to the truth positive oils have robust aromas.

You should be capable of find out the oils that sense most natural to you thru this sampling, similarly to the ones that elicit specific emotions in you. People frequently select out the perfume of cinnamon with the holiday season, as I already indicated, and the identical is true with the fragrance of pine bushes and campfires. Although there isn't always an vital oil for campfires, there may be one for pine wood and for quite a good deal some other season or interest you might imagine.

What are vital oils precisely?

Typically, an important oil is a liquid that has been distilled from a plant. Water from a pass or slowly flowing river is typically blended with the leaves, flowers, stems, bark, and different factors of the plant this is used to make this unique oil in some unspecified time in the future of the distillation manner. Contrary to popular notion, crucial oils do not without a doubt have an oily experience. Most critical oils are transparent or extremely easy sun solar sunglasses of orange or amber. The real essence of the plant or tree from which they have been derived is idea to be covered in important oils. The vital oils are often supplied in quite small bottles that could closing a completely long time due to the fact they keep a immoderate attention.

While critical oils do include odors, they are no longer much like or perhaps near perfumes or different types of fragrances. While the big majority of fragrance or fragrance oils are synthetically produced or no a lot less than encompass synthetic materials and often have little to no medicinal impact, vital oils are constantly obtained from actual flowers. Many companies will sell it perfume oils as aromatherapy recovery oils however the reality that they're not the same due to the fact the use of the time period aromatherapy isn't but regulated by way of way of the American government. This is unhappy due to the fact those aromatic oils often incorporate little or no herbal additives. It is vital to understand that if an aromatherapy product includes any kind of artificial or fragrance oil, it isn't actually an aromatherapy product and is instead being bought as such.

The thriller to therapeutic essential oils is their fragrance and chemical makeup. This technique that perfume and chemical composition need to have huge restoration effects at the body at the equal time as moreover lowering highbrow anxiety. The majority of folks who use recuperation oils attain this through inhalation and special pores and pores and skin applications that use diluted oil.

Principal crucial oils

Essential oils are to be had in a large shape of office paintings, and every one has unique traits. Many of these oils are applied in cooking in awesome paperwork—you may no longer even be privy to it! In a special form (such leaves or powdered powder), you would possibly find out some of the following important oils in normal circle of relatives cooking:

Basil

Because of its extremely good taste, basil is regularly utilized in cooking for masses of functions. It has licorice-like, candy, herbaceous, and aromatic features. Despite the reality that basil is maximum regularly carried out in cooking, it is able to additionally be used to remedy lots of ailments, which encompass bronchitis, colds, coughs, exhaustion, flatulence, the flu, gout, laptop virus bites, rheumatism, and sinusitis. Basil need to exceptional be implemented sparingly and punctiliously, despite the fact that. Basil incorporates methyl chavicol, which has been connected to most cancers whilst consumed in more. It is suggested that you keep away from the use of basil if you have liver issues and that you keep away from the usage of basil even as pregnant.

Ginger

Another aromatherapy crucial oil is ginger, that is frequently carried out in cooking. It smells heat, exceedingly spiced, earthy, and vegetal. The excellent makes use of for ginger consist of the consolation of aching muscle tissues, arthritis, nausea, and terrible circulate. If you will be inside the solar for a extended amount of time, you need to now not use this due to the reality it may reason sun poisoning.

Lemon

Most human beings are familiar with lemons due to the fact they're a instead commonplace fruit. Its aroma resembles that of lemon rinds, however it's far richer and more potent. Athlete's foot, chilblains, colds, corns, dull pores and pores and skin, flu, oily skin, spots, varicose veins, and warts can all be dealt with with it. Lemon need to also no longer be fed on if you may be in direct daylight hours for a extended quantity of time, much like the recommendation for ginger.

Parsley

Frequently finished in cooking is parsley. It has a robust, woodsy fragrance that is from time to time pretty attractive. Amenorrhea, arthritis, cellulites, cystitis, frigidity, griping pains, indigestion, rheumatism, and toxic buildup are a few of the conditions it's miles frequently used to treat. But once in a while, this particular vital oil may be risky. It regularly reasons liver toxicity and can purpose abortions. Extreme warning should be exercised at the same time as the use of it anywhere, mainly round pregnant ladies.

Peppermint

You're truly quite acquainted with the smell of peppermint, it is quite regular. It has a sturdy spearmint flavor, however it is stronger and fragrant. People often partner this aroma with the Christmas season. Asthma, colic, tiredness, fever, flatulence, headache, nausea, scabies, sinusitis, and vertigo can all be correctly treated with it. It need to be avoided if you have epilepsy or a fever because of the truth it is able to be mildly poisonous in your nerves. It is viable to consume peppermint orally, but fine with the help of a knowledgeable aromatherapy expert.

Thyme

Cooks often employ thyme of their recipes. It smells glowing however moreover medicinal. Thyme is often used to cope with a whole lot of conditions, collectively with arthritis, dermatitis, laryngitis, lice, muscle aches, terrible go along with the flow, scabies, sore throats, and computer virus stings. Thyme should not be utilized by those who have immoderate blood stress. It also can moreover worsen the pores and skin or be a powerful mucous membrane irritant.

Rose

The use of rose in aromatherapy is mainly captivating. We are all acquainted with receiving flora as objects. However, aromatherapy additionally uses roses. They scent adorable and delicious. Rose is frequently used to address melancholy, eczema, frigidity, aged pores and pores and skin, menopause, and pressure in the form of critical oils. Remember that even the fragrance of roses can assist to alleviate anxiety and despair while you don't forget giving someone you care approximately a bouquet of pink roses. Why do ladies adore them lots?

Nutmeg

The majority of humans are very familiar with nutmeg. It smells great, rich, exceedingly spiced, sweet, and woodsy. The cooking spice's important oil can be very similar to it, even though it is richer and extra aromatic. It is often used to deal with rheumatism, constipation, gradual digestion, weariness, muscle aches, nausea, and neuralgia.

Marjoram

In assessment to the opportunity spices defined here, marjoram is not used as frequently in cuisine. Its fine and woodsy aroma in aromatherapy can be pretty beautiful. It is capable of handling pretty some potential troubles and although smells pinnacle. It is used to remedy ticks, sprains, traces, excessive blood strain, aching muscle mass, amenorrhea, bronchitis, chilblains, colic, coughing, immoderate sex pressure, flatulence, and ticks. There aren't any extra protection precautions required, however pregnant ladies need to keep away from using it.

Lavender

The French chemist Gattefosse found aromatherapy after taking an unintentional dose of lavender oil, as became formerly defined within the history of the exercise. What precisely does lavender deal with? Its fragrant features—glowing, sweet, flowery, and barely fruity—are especially seemed. There are a big sort of situations for which it is able to be used, at the facet of pimples, allergies, tension, allergies, athlete's foot, bruises, burns, fowl pox, colic, cuts, cystitis, depression, dermatitis, dysmenorrhea, earache, flatulence, headache, high blood pressure, itching, labor pains, migraine, oily pores and skin, rheumatism, scabies, scars, sores, sprains, There aren't any particular protection measures required on the same time as the usage of this critical oil, irrespective of all of its severa treatments.

Safety of critical oils

When the usage of crucial oils, it's far essential which you use protection and caution, similar to with all treatments, pills, and remedies. Keep in mind that those are quite centered beverages that, if no longer used efficaciously or as directed, might be unstable. But do not be alarmed by way of that. You have to prevail with aromatherapy so long as you use prudence and keep understanding.

In the case of precise oils, protection precautions can on occasion be ignored with the advice of an experienced and geared up aromatherapy practitioner. When doubtful, please talk along with your clinical medical doctor or an aromatherapy expert who has surpassed via suitable training.

A important rule to preserve in thoughts is that important oils should in no way be executed to the pores and pores and skin undiluted. Although there might be a few exceptions to this precaution, you need to in no manner make that decision with out carefully consulting a topic-rely expert. When executed to the pores and pores and skin, the oil can be quite poisonous, aggravate the pores and skin, and purpose rashes and extreme sensitivity. Tea tree and lavender may be carried out to the pores and skin, however this have to simplest be performed very on occasion to keep away from the danger of sensitivity.

Remember that a few people may additionally additionally moreover experience sensitive or allergies to positive oils. Some people are going to be allergic to the important oils utilized in aromatherapy, similar to they may be to practically the entirety else. Apply a totally small amount of diluted vital oil (in no way undiluted) to a small patch of pores and pores and skin to shield yourself and others in opposition to a potential allergy. Applying Band-Aid after doing this to the indoors of the elbow may be beneficial. Check to peer if there can be any type of response with the beneficial useful resource of letting the oil sit down down down for at least 24 hours. No matter how assured you are that you won't react adversely to any important oil, you have to usually take a look at first.

Some vital oils also can reason troubles for parents which are pregnant, have bronchial asthma, epilepsy, or one-of-a-type severe medical issues. To keep away from difficulties, maintain this in mind and check the vital oil's warnings in advance than the usage of it to a person who also can already be experiencing a health problem.

Never use crucial oils orally until specially told to perform that via a scientific scientific doctor or licensed aromatherapy expert. Only some few oils, at great, regulated quantities, can be fed on orally. These should only be taken as directed thru a medical physician or certified aromatherapist.

Essential oils, now not just like the majority of factors in life, usually adhere to the maxim "tons much less is extra." Just enough essential oil ought to be used to complete the mission. Because important oils are so targeted, it in all fairness clean to apply an excessive amount of of them.

The use of crucial oils for aromatherapy isn't suitable for they all. If used in any respect, unique critical oils like wormwood, pennyroyal, onion, camphor, horseradish, wintergreen, rue, sour almond, and sassafras ought to constantly be administered under the steering of a professional aromatherapy expert.

Remember that flammable essential oils exist! When using critical oils near flames, you need to typically take utmost warning to avoid a fireplace.

It need to pass with out pronouncing that youngsters have to in no way use crucial oils with out an person who is knowledgeable in aromatherapy present. By making sure that children can't get right of entry on your crucial oil deliver, you may avoid forgetting to take this precaution. Keep them out of children's obtain and in a solid location.

Harmful oils

Some oils are regarded as harmful and dangerous. Oil isn't always continually innocent or without any negative outcomes that you have to be privy to clearly as it is not listed right here as being volatile. Just be cautious and do your homework earlier than using any important oils.

Ajowan (Trachyspermum copticum)

Almond, Bitter (Prunus dulcis var. Amara)

Arnica (Arnica Montana)

Birch, Sweet (Betula lenta)

Boldo Leaf (Peumus boldus) Broom, Spanish (Spartium junceum)

Calamus (Acorus calamus var. Angustatus)

Camphor (Cinnamomum camphora)

Deertongue (Carphephorus odoratissimus)

Garlic (Allium sativum) Horseradish (Armoracia rusticana) Jaborandi (Pilocarpus jaborandi)

Melilotus (Melilotus officinalis)

Mugwort (Artemisia vulgaris)

Mustard (Brassica nigra)

Onion (Allium cepa)

Pennyroyal (Mentha pulegium)

Rue (Ruta graveolens)

Sassafras (Sassafras albidum)

Thuja (Thuja occidentalis) Wintergreen (Gaultheria procumbens)

Wormseed (Chenopodium ambrosioides var. Anthelminticum) Wormwood (Artemisia absinthium)

Here is a listing of volatile oils to stay far from, listed in alphabetical order:

Once more, regardless of the truth that at the same time as this listing carries oils which is probably dangerous in fashionable, it does not suggest that there aren't any extra risky oils or oils with capability issue consequences that might damage you, mainly if you have already were given a scientific hassle.

Chapter 7: How To Use Thoroughly

Can I supply aromatherapy to my doggy?

Aromatherapy also can additionally gain humans, and it can moreover advantage our dogs with the aid of giving them the vital healing (each emotional and recuperation) consequences. But it's far essential to keep in thoughts that animals and people are very particular from every other. It is in fact useful to speak with an authorized aromatherapist who has experience jogging with animals and is comfortable doing so. "Holistic Aromatherapy for Animals" by way of the use of Kristen Leigh Bell, published in 2002, is a suggested ebook at the project. The only great supply on the effects of aromatherapy on animals is this ebook.

Is kid's aromatherapy stable?

Remember that almost all of the recipes and commands for aromatherapy which can be now available are designed for everyday, healthful, average-sized humans under the supervision of a clinical expert in case you plan to apply it with your children. Any recipes intended to be used with youngsters have to name for a much decrease dosage than the same old recipe may also. Certain oils ought to in no way be used on kids. In this example, it's far pleasant to be cautious, and you need to constantly use caution and care on the identical time as administering aromatherapy treatments to youngsters.

Neroli, rose, candy orange, tea tree, lavender, and roman chamomile are some oils which can be regularly solid to use round kids in modest dosages. It is high-quality to are looking for for recommendation from a informed man or woman in these topics because of the reality youngsters want to have unique problems made for their age, period, weight, and goals.

Is aromatherapy secure to apply at the equal time as pregnant?

This is a hotly contested situation depend. Many humans disagree that aromatherapy need to be used in the course of pregnancy because the capability detrimental outcomes are sometimes doubtful and there may be little interest in "trying out" this to see whether or no longer or no longer aromatherapy may also want to have a damaging impact on fetuses. While a few humans suggest the use of particular oils, it's miles really actual that certain oils must in no way be used by a pregnant girl.

Some oils would possibly cause uterine contractions or spontaneous abortions. Other oils are complicated due to the fact they're awful for diabetics, and a few pregnant ladies increase the disease. However, it is unknown if those oils have been achieved because it have to be and properly at the time the incidents passed off.

Since it's far risky to adopt this form of locating out on humans, maximum of this look at has been completed on animals. Researchers have, but, been able to pinpoint some oils which might be seemed to result in pregnancy-associated issues. These encompass:

Benzoin

Bergamot

Grapefruit

Lavender   Lemon

Neroli

Orange

Patchouli   Sandalwood

Spearmint

Tea Tree

Vetiver

If you are watching for or assume you is probably pregnant, stay away from the ones oils. Finding options and being secure are heaps advanced to being sorry later.

Some aromatherapy oils, despite the fact that, are steady for expectant moms. For instance, notwithstanding the fact that they'll be now not advocated for use within the direction of the real being pregnant, jasmine, clary sage, and rose have a propensity to be very beneficial at a few diploma within the actual begin. It is right to have an aromatherapist who's licensed layout a combination specially on the way to take in some unspecified time in the future of delivery with the intention to lessen the discomfort, pressure, and worrying situations.

Chapter 8: Carrier Oils

What are Carrier Oils?

Another issue of aromatherapy treatment is company oils. Although they are often called base oils or vegetable oils, they serve a miles wider type of talents. Before utilizing crucial oils, CO2s, and absolutes for your pores and pores and skin, issuer oils are used to dilute them. This allows you to take an essential oil that has already been diluted and mix it with a base oil or company oil, at which factor it will possibly be seemed as diluted. You can then efficaciously use it on your pores and pores and skin as a give up result.

Different corporation oils have precise tendencies that would both enhance the healing consequences of the vital oil you're using or offer restoration advantages in their personal. Typically, cold-pressed vegetable oils derived from the fatty factors of precise vegetation are used to cause them to. They do no longer evaporate or deliver the critical oils their private flavor. Strangely, provider oils can lose their efficiency. Common provider oils will lose their performance through the years, but vital oils can undergo simply all of the time. You want to both use herbal food regimen E as a preservative or have herbal carrier oils.

Carrier oil examples and applications?

Carrier oils are available a wide kind of sorts. Here are maximum of the company oils that are applied more often.

Almond oil

Cooking using olive oil isn't always uncommon. Its herbal perfume, which I will talk over with as having an olive fragrance, is extraordinarily much like that of cooking oil. It has a heavy, greasy feel and a mild to medium inexperienced tint. It is important to apply a small or ok amount in dilution due to the fact a bigger amount must overshadow the aggregate.

Almond oil

A little or no nuttiness may be detected in the peanut oil's quite moderate heady scent. It is form of smooth in colour, has a thick texture, and leaves a virtually greasy layer at the pores and pores and skin. Peanut oil should now not be used on anybody who is allergic to peanuts, therefore use caution at the same time as using it. Due to its oily texture and functionality to help with arthritis, it's far regularly a totally suitable desire to apply with rub down oils or in a rubdown combination.

Almond oil, sweet

The fragrance of candy almond oil is sensitive, really sweet, and nutty. Although it is barely greasy and will depart the pores and skin feeling oily, it dissipates unexpectedly. Although nearly easy, it has a touch of yellow. Since sweet almond oil is a flexible service oil that works nicely with nearly any critical oil and is fairly priced, it's far a fantastic possibility for almost all of essential oils.

Oil from Cocoa Butter

Rich and sweet, the aroma of cocoa butter oil is unmistakably just like that of chocolate. At room temperature, this form of butter although stands corporation and difficult and crumbles. At a moderate or warmth, it is an useful oil for heating and easing. It has a mild tan shade. To be useful, cocoa butter oil wants to be blended with different materials or oils. It is a high-quality oil to include into creams and creams.

Almond Oil

The aroma of hazelnut oil is touchy, nutty, and comparatively candy. It leaves a completely faint oily feeling and is skinny. Because it does no longer leave nearly as plenty of an oily residue as one-of-a-kind company oils can, it's far very useful for people with oily pores and skin. Because it would not leave an oily residue, clients might not experience zits flare-the us often, which is probably a not unusual hassle inside the United States and a few place else because of products that depart oily residue and makeup.

Canola Oil

Pecan oil leaves best a touch oily movie at the pores and skin, has a medium viscosity, and a subtly fatty and nutty aroma. Although it is nearly obvious in color, it's miles believed to damage right away. In order to preserve it from deteriorating from exposure to sunshine, it want to be saved in a darkish-coloured bottle in a darkish area.

You can appoint a significant variety of numerous carrier oils, each of which has a completely unique feature, aroma, texture, and colour. Although no longer entire, this listing does provide you with a notable idea of the styles of oils you might be able to use to dilute your important oils.

Chapter 9: Other Resources About Absolutes

Essential oils and absolutes percentage many similarities. They are liquids which have been derived from plant fabric and are quite fragrant. However, the way absolutes are collected from their herbal sources is what makes them exceptional from essential oils. Chemical solvents must be used, but they'll be eliminated during the last tiers of manufacture.

Absolutes are frequently more intensely focused than their vital oil opposite numbers. If you make use of aromatherapy for relaxation or as a medical remedy, it's miles vital that you comprise crucial recovery oils into your private routine.

The top notch drawback of the use of or producing absolutes is the opportunity of traces of the chemical solvent final within the finished product. There isn't any way to assure that each one of the chemical solvent has been taken out of absolutely the sooner than it enters the final venture degrees, therefore that is without a doubt unavoidable. Because they had to be extracted the use of chemical solvents, absolutes are not absolutely natural, it's far why many people best use them from time to time.

Another massive distinction among crucial oils and absolutes is that it isn't counseled for everybody who isn't always sufficiently knowledgeable, expert, and expert to take vital oils internally. Absolutes, as a substitute, want to in no way be taken internally irrespective of who you are, making this example even more excessive. This is a given for the purpose that absolutes contain traces of chemical substance.

About Hydrosols

Another element that may be applied in aromatherapy remedies is hydrosols. The water this is left over after an vital oil is extracted from plant cloth is called a hydrosol. This is frequently referred to as distillate water or floral water. When critical oils are extracted from plant fabric, the water itself alternatives up part of the medicinal traits and adorable fragrance of the oil. Hydrosols, however, are thru-merchandise of the distillation device.

About Resins

Resins can be a phrase you're already familiar with. When a tree is damage, a cloth called resin spontaneously develops. Trees produce resin, that's a thick, stable substance that sticks to itself if the bark is penetrated. Making collectible collectible figurines or other accumulating gadgets is surely one of the many uses for this resin.

Naturally taking region resins made thru wood do have restoration advantages. However, due to the truth those resins are thick and sticky, running with them can be difficult. Resins may be located in liquid shape after being extracted with a solvent or alcohol technique.

About CO2s

CO2s are oils that have lengthy past thru a first rate extraction technique. Carbon dioxide is used on this way. Pressure is finished to carbon dioxide until it liquidizes. When applied to natural plant be counted, it may then be executed as a solvent, and the additives of the plant that might have produced vital oil dissolve into the liquid CO_2. The aggregate is afterwards pulled back as much as its unique kingdom, at which issue the CO_2 debris vaporize into gaseous form, leaving the ensuing oil in the lower back of.

Because no traces of any poisonous solvent or chemical are left within the finished product, CO2s are frequently taken into consideration as being just like important oils. The effectiveness of the oil isn't lessened through this technique both. CO2s commonly have a thicker consistency and scent more similar to the unique plant cloth. They are often current as an improved product.

About Uninfused Oils

Infused oil is a considered one of a type type of oil that is regularly hired in aromatherapy. The oils from plant material are extracted in a one-of-a-type manner for infused oil. In this extraction method, one or extra herbs are infused into a provider oil. This sort of oil possesses the dispositions of a company oil in addition to the recovery functions of the oil itself and the herbs which have been infused into it.

While many plants have recovery or recuperation traits, no longer all of these species may be converted into vital oils. This is because of the reality that they do no longer encompass enough oil to allow for an crucial oil to be extracted from them. To make infused oil, you will but infuse that specific plant or herb with a company oil. Depending on the lowest oil, infused oils will be inclined to be exceptionally greasy. They can degrade through the years and are manifestly diluted due to the truth they had been combined with the provider oil. Even at home, the usage of a crock top and a very low warmth putting, you could create infused oil. When making your very very own infused oil, you ought to be fairly cautious because it is easy to overheat the oil.

Chapter 10: Promoting Emotional Well-Being With Aromatherapy

The use of crucial oils in aromatherapy, in particular, can be quite effective in fostering a sturdy enjoy of emotional properly-being. It can assist the improvement of wholesome emotional states and aid the selection of troubles like sadness, rage, or frustration. People who often sense pressured out might imagine approximately using important oils to help create a much less annoying environment and to assist them lighten up.

Because important oils are made of compounds that obviously get up in plant rely and can be delivered in a synergistic way, aromatherapy is in particular powerful in this case. Because their molecules are easy to breathe in, they might act straight away and input the body rapid.

Certain additives of the thoughts can be inspired and impacted thru the chemicals launched in a few unspecified time in the future of aromatherapy. The mind may be stimulated via those triggers to produce tremendous emotions or to squelch others. Naturally, now not clearly anyone can be impacted with the aid of crucial oils in the same way. The emotional effects of an aroma might also additionally vary counting on different recollections that humans have approximately specific aromas.

For instance, the capability of an oil or fragrance to favorably have an effect for your emotional well being is probably impacted if you revel in a specifically robust emotional reaction to it. You are tons much less probably to be pleasantly tormented by cinnamon if the fine and comfortable and comforting aroma, that is typically associated with cinnamon, has emerge as related to the passing of a member of the family.

What critical oils have an effect on highbrow health?

Aromatherapy practitioners have the view that it has a superb impact on and great impact on someone's emotional well being.

Humans experience a amazing kind of emotional states, and which will maintain contributing to society, we need to address the ones feelings. Grief makes it tough to have interaction with others, and rage makes it an increasing number of tougher.

As a quit stop result, some human beings use aromatherapy as a manner of dealing with those immoderate emotions. Various oils have developments that address severa emotional states.

The majority of human emotions that we need to every stifle or beautify are blanketed within the list underneath.

Anger

Bergamot, Jasmine, Neroli,

Orange, Patchouli, Petitgrain,

Roman Chamomile, Rose,

Vetiver, Ylang Ylang

Anxiety

Bergamot, Cedarwood, Clary

Sage, Frankincense, Geranium,

Lavender, Mandarin, Neroli,

Patchouli, Roman Chamomile,

Rose, Sandalwood, Vetiver

Confidence

Bay Laurel, Bergamot, Cypress,

Grapefruit, Jasmine, Orange, Rosemary

Depression

Bergamot, Clary Sage,

Frankincense, Geranium,

Grapefruit, Helichrysum,

Jasmine, Lavender, Lemon,

Mandarin, Neroli, Orange, Roman Chamomile,
Rose, Sandalwood, Ylang Ylang

Fatigue, Exhaustion and Burnout

Basil, Bergamot, Black Pepper,

Clary Sage, Cypress,

Frankincense, Ginger,

Grapefruit, Helichrysum,

Jasmine, Lemon, Patchouli,

Peppermint, Rosemary,

Sandalwood, Vetiver

Fear

Bergamot, Cedarwood, Clary

Sage, Frankincense, Grapefruit,

Jasmine, Lemon, Neroli,

Orange, Roman Chamomile

Sandalwood, Vetiver

Grief

Cypress, Frankincense,

Helichrysum, Neroli, Rose, Sandalwood, Vetiver

Happiness and Peace

Bergamot, Frankincense,

Geranium, Grapefruit, Lemon,

Neroli, Orange, Rose,

Sandalwood, Ylang Ylang

Insecurity

Bergamot, Cedarwood,

Frankincense, Jasmine, Sandalwood, Vetiver

Irritability

Lavender, Mandarin, Neroli,

Roman Chamomile, Sandalwood

Loneliness

Bergamot, Clary Sage,

Frankincense, Helichrysum, Roman Chamomile, Rose

Memory and Concentration

Basil, Black Pepper, Cypress,

Hyssop, Lemon, Peppermint, Rosemary

Panic and Panic Attacks

Frankincense, Helichrysum,

Lavender, Neroli, Rose

Stress

Benzoin, Bergamot, Clary Sage,

Frankincense, Geranium,

Grapefruit, Jasmine, Lavender,

Mandarin, Neroli, Patchouli, Roman Chamomile, Rose,

Sandalwood, Vetiver, Ylang

Ylang

How can aromatherapy fight melancholy?

Depression is frequently introduced on by using using hormonal, pharmacological, or situational factors, or each. Death of a loved one, bodily or verbal abuse, financial troubles, relocating, loneliness, retirement, unemployment, divorce, or strain in existence are examples of "situational" triggers. The majority of the time, despair is brief and fades fast, but it may moreover ultimate for drastically longer in one in all a kind cases.

Always are searching out the recommendation of a licensed health practitioner if you expect you will be depressed a high-quality manner to remedy the ones problems. You should probably want to start taking remedy, and she or he will probable propose treatment. It is higher to cope with depression below a medical doctor's steering.

Keep in thoughts that aromatherapy is pleasant supplemental if you choose out to utilize it to deal with your depression. Aromatherapy can be very useful for boosting your sizeable mood and attitude on lifestyles, however it can not update clinical treatment for despair, especially at the same time as it is introduced on with the useful resource of hormonal or chemical imbalances.

To decorate your enjoy of fitness, you may employ aromatherapy. Try the usage of an aromatherapy air freshener or room spray inside the path of the day, a diffuser (like a reed diffuser wherein the oils climb a reed and diffuse into the air), a massage with aromatherapy lotions (even a self-massage using aromatherapy oils can be so smooth), and pores and skin and hair aromatherapy products. Your day may be easier and you can enjoy less forced and stressful as your senses are uncovered to the restoration consequences of the oils at some point of the day. Bath salts and oils are similarly options.

Chapter 11: Is Aromatherapy Effective For Weight Loss?

When it involves assisting humans shed kilos, aromatherapy has been a hotly contested problem. Every feasible technique of weight reduction has been explored given that absolutely everyone is looking for a quick remedy for weight problems. There has been a few achievement with aromatherapy, although it varies, as it does with all elements of the exercising.

Before developing any weight loss plans for yourself, as with all weight loss applications, you need to talk with a scientific physician or one in all a kind healthcare professional. Working with an expert in this place is generally encouraged to make sure that a technique is created that mainly fits your desires.

Naturally, using critical oils may not motive you to shed pounds right now. No depend what they're announcing, not anything will cause you to lose weight in a paranormal way.

However, aromatherapy will let you experience a good buy a good deal less hungry and plenty a great deal much less willing to eat extra meals, if you want to reduce your urge to devour. Additionally, it's going to let you have extra power on the same time as exercise and experience plenty much less exhausted, so that you can make you need to rise up and exercising more. It is important to live on a schedule whilst trying to shed kilos, so hold this in thoughts at the same time as growing your personal exercise plan. Any weight loss plan wishes consuming the exceptional meals and doing masses of exercising. Everything else you embody on your diet plan is surely supplemental that will help you in carrying out your critical objective.

Chapter 12: Essential Oil Blending

The functionality of vital oils to be mixed in order to elicit specific reactions from folks that is probably exposed to them is one in all their remarkable and captivating tendencies. You can without issues make your very very very own crucial oil mixture to make a adorable scented combination for both non-public enjoyment and domestic perfume. Additionally, crucial oils may be combined therapeutically to assist lighten up muscular tissues, reduce strain, or improve happiness. Aromatic and recuperation functions are the two critical justifications for combining critical oils.

The aroma of the completed product is the primary attention in aromatic combinations. While a few aromatic combos have medicinal houses, the cause is to offer a selected fragrance or perfume for a given use. Only natural substances like absolutes, grain alcohol, provider oils, essential oils, water, or herbs need to be carried out.

A woodsy, earthy, quite spiced, citrus, flowery, medicinal, minty, peppery, or Oriental aroma are most of the maximum common aromas that human beings try and create. Analyze the aromatic tendencies of the vital oils you advise to use to make certain they won't struggle with each exceptional too much. Additionally, this can assist you turn out to be privy to whether or not critical oils have a highly spiced, minty, or woodsy scent.

However, to be able to create a top-notch series, you aren't required to stick to the same kind or qualification of perfume. For example, so long as they're not overbearing, floral, Oriental, or citrus oils often pair pretty properly with exceptionally spiced and Oriental oils. When putting together an oil combination, go through in mind that floral oils normally move thoroughly with rather spiced, citrus, and woodsy oils as nicely. These oils can also furthermore promote more relaxation and enhance treatment for you. There are many numerous mixtures that may be executed; to determine which one will art work brilliant for you, it's miles extremely good to strive masses of superb aromatherapy combinations first.

The recuperation effect of the aggregate is the precept hobby in restoration blends. These mixtures are supposed to useful useful resource in each a bodily or mental circumstance. You want to combine oils with the favored healing outcomes (collectively with, to deal with bronchial bronchial asthma). You can combine numerous important oils that have been counseled for treating bronchial allergic reactions. This need to now not be used as your number one approach of remedy for bronchial bronchial asthma; as a substitute, you have to use your inhaler as quick as you enjoy signs and signs and symptoms, found thru aromatherapy to help reduce the severity of the assault and prevent further ones.

Additionally, you can combine vital oils with severa homes to remedy situations like a combination of bronchial allergic reactions, hypertension, arthritis, and insomnia. Just be cautious not to combine it with any crucial oils that would harm your health, and use intense caution when you have a peanut hypersensitivity or are pregnant.

Also maintain in thoughts that a few essential oils might also additionally energize you at the equal time as others may want to make you sleepy. Avoid the usage of oils that would positioned you to sleep in case you need to utilize them in advance than your day even gets going. This additionally works the other way, so be careful not to use stimulating oils swiftly earlier than bed. Doing so may also additionally keep you up for the maximum of the night time time and prevent you from being sufficiently rested to go back to art work the following morning.

It's a wonderful method to cater for your desires especially to combine oils to remedy various illnesses or medical conditions. Just be careful while developing your blends and keep away from including an excessive amount of of any oil as a manner to overshadow the others within the combination and make it more difficult if you want to sense their outcomes.

How to combo

There aren't any set suggestions for blending critical oils to create a selected fragrance or healing mixture. When blending your oils, there are a few critical recommendations that you could need to preserve in thoughts. Starting with fewer drops of every kind of oil permit you to avoid dropping any unneeded oil, for that reason it is advocated to gain this. Additionally, it's going to assist you in locating out whether or not or now not more is an awful lot a whole lot less or lots plenty much less is greater and deciding on the approach that is top notch for you.

Starting your aggregate with most effective crucial oils, absolutes, or CO_2s is usually endorsed. If critical, you could then dilute it with additional service oils or alcohol, as a manner to help you avoid dropping any of your alcohol or provider oils. Make excessive first-class to keep an extensive listing of all the oils you operate, on the factor of the quantity of drops you use for each oil. It is surely too easy to get carried away and forget about to put in writing down the ones thorough notes, but you may want them to breed your paintings later or to make the recipe better if you decide to alternate some element.

Make amazing to thoroughly label every aggregate so you are aware about what it is, what it's miles used for, and what factors it consists of. You may think about labeling your mixture in a few exclusive way and keeping that label along the recipe in a magazine of a few type. Use vital oils with a mild hand if the aroma isn't overbearing. If now not carried out within the right mixture, a few aromas may be more potent than others and can overshadow the others. Before combining the oils with others, you will in all likelihood choice to attempt with them on their private to get a sense of the way extremely good the aroma and potential results are.

It isn't always a incredible concept to throw away your combination even in case you do now not find it irresistible straight away away. The mixture ought to be saved for a time so that you can also come again to it later. Your combination's elements may additionally on occasion want a while to meld before the preferred perfume can be elicited. In addition, you'll possibly get used to it! It's moreover feasible which you have been uncovered to too many awesome fragrances in advance than your "questionable" product grow to be completed, making it hard to as it need to be come across the proper aroma.

Chapter 13: The Use Of Diffusers

You can use a diffuser as a "tool" to help in assisting the molecules of an important oil to diffuse into the air. The diffuser lets in you to take gain of the advantages of aromatherapy on the equal time as breathing in regular air.

Tissues

Diffusion via a tissue or handkerchief is one of the maximum sincere strategies. The tissue has very tiny drips of the oil on it, however it's going to deliver the molecules with it anywhere you go with the flow. It is pretty discreet and portable, and it is able to results be tucked right into a pocket and carried spherical with you at some stage in the day.

Diffusion of Steam

Diffusion of steam is each other method. You can put together a bowl of water with the aid of way of boiling a few cups of water. The oil can be poured into the basin in a few droplets. The water will hold to release steam into the air because of the fact it's far already warm. The important oils will now be carried thru manner of the steam, that could be a enjoyable cause to attempt the usage of aromatherapy. It also can be an appropriate accompaniment to a spa or rub down session.

Using a Candle

With this approach, you slight a candle and allow it burn for a brief at the same time as. After a brief while, extinguish the candle, upload a drop of oil to the wax that has melted, after which relight it. Because vital oils are enormously flamable, exercising severe warning. To prevent them from catching fireplace, preserve the oil in the wax and a ways from the flames.

Dispersion of Reeds

An increasingly commonplace diffusion technique is this one. This approach includes dipping a reed right into a basin of diluted vital oils. The oil substance is absorbed with the aid of manner of the reed, and the liquid flows up the reed. The oil vapors disperse into the air as the liquid flows.

Blower Diffusion

This is likewise extremely effective. In this method, an essential oil is subtle into the air the usage of a fan diffuser. A disposable pad or tray is inserted in the larger tool, and the fan blows across it. Oil specks are lifted into the air through the air that the fan blows across the tray.

Other Approaches

Diffusers are to be had in a large sort of particular kinds. They range in phrases of length, complexity, and the depth of the perfume this is emitted into the distance. While a few are less hard to address an entire room, others are greater intimate that allows you to keep in your person. It is vital to assess the numerous diffuser types a exquisite way to determine which one is suitable for your reason because of the truth a few will produce extra concentrations than others.

Chapter 14: Storing Essential Oils

Significant oils do not expire, that is an vital trouble to maintain in thoughts. Therefore, if you take some right precautions, preserving them can be quite clean. They are regularly available in small bottles, however you may locate certainly one of a type sized bottles to apply in case you're generating your very very own blends (maintain in mind that in case your mixture has a perishable oil in it, this limits your capacity to save it).

While critical oils do not lose their overall performance, they might degrade and lose their usefulness. Not all oils will oxidize and lose their medicinal houses in addition to their perfume. The perfect field for your oils is one that is translucent but no longer obvious.

The finest bottles for this are those which may be amber or blue considering they may diffuse any slight that attempts to enter the oils. All of your aromatherapy merchandise, in particular those which could spark off phototoxicity for the cause that they'll be extra liable to the damaging outcomes of mild, need to continuously be saved below dark glass.

In fact, the usage of darkish glass is such a problem that you need to not purchase any oils which might be advertised in clean packing containers. You won't be able to tell how lengthy this oil turned into saved in a obvious bottle, and it might have already lost a number of its efficacy due to exposure to mild. Pay interest to bins with rubber stoppers as well. Although it can appear very accessible, a rubber stopper want to in no manner be positioned within the bottle itself for the reason that it could grow to be sticky from the very focused oil. You won't boom get entry to oil outbreaks in case you keep this oil in a bottle. The truth that metal bottles may be used for storage as long as they will be covered on the internal is every other vital reality to be aware about. You want to not employ something that isn't always protected.

Keep your essential oils in a dim, shaded region wherein they won't be exposed to direct daylight hours and at a low temperature (no longer refrigerated or frozen). The satisfactory technique to make sure they last as long as viable is to do that. Your oils may also smash due to deterioration that is elevated by using warmness and daytime.

Chapter 15: The Skinny On Essential Oils

Long earlier than multilevel advertising and advertising companies presented vital oils via the pound, historical healers and botanists were harnessing the goodness of nature in a number of tactics. Using plant fabric in numerous techniques, those human beings located treatment options for complications, low mood, horrible sleep, and other maladies lengthy earlier than the contemporary pharmaceutical enterprise superior. One of the earliest use times of essential oils can be traced to 3000 BCE. Botanists and physicians placed in China, Egypt, and India made use of plenty of essences and oils for drugs and perfumes (Chitwood, 2020). It became additionally believed that the strong heady scent of oils had beneficial outcomes beyond perfumery. In this economic destroy, we'll take a higher test what vital oils are, empower you to choose out expired oils, and percent vital safety guidelines.

So what are vital oils? The handiest explanation is that they'll be extracts of the flowers' fragrant essences. Plants produce aromatic essences for hundreds motives, collectively with attracting pollinators, repelling predators, and discouraging competition from close by plant life. These essences assist to maintain the plant blanketed and healthful. Collecting the ones oils is a complex organization, with four strategies being used.

Steam Distillation

This is the maximum commonplace and oldest approach of crucial oil manufacturing. Here, steam passes through a hopper containing raw plant cloth, liberating the fragrant compounds. These compounds vaporize and upward push with the steam proper right into a cooling gadget and condenser. From there, the plant essences and water aggregate is separated into essential oil and floral water. This approach of extraction makes use of numerous warmth, making it fallacious to be used on tremendous botanicals.

Expression

It is a likely assumption that maximum people have taken a citrus peel and squeezed it, ensuing in a extraordinary spray of oil. That is surely how citrus oils are extracted! The peels are prepared (usually pricked or soaked in warm water) and then mechanically pressed. From there, the pulpy liquid is popped right into a centrifuge and separated into juice and important oil. This is the cold-urgent technique of extraction and is a considerably charge-powerful method, specially as regards to the manufacturing of lemon, orange, and one of a kind citrus vital oils. A large problem right right here is possible contamination from pesticides, making it pretty vital to move the herbal route whilst seeking out vital oils.

Solvent Extraction

Many aromatics are not technically taken into consideration important oils and are obtained with the aid of the use of solvents like hexane, supercritical carbon dioxide, or dimethyl ether in the extraction techniques (Villafranco, 2018). Depending at the solvent used, the toxicity and residue created may be negligible. Carbon dioxide extraction is gaining in reputation and is considered to be the least poisonous solvent to apply. The approach is pretty interesting and includes setting a chamber complete of plant material and carbon dioxide underneath excessive pressure. The concept is to expose the carbon dioxide proper into a dense fog, which lets in the fragrant components of the plant material to dissolve. When the fuel is separated from the cloth, it leaves handiest the extracted fragrant essences of the plant at the back of it. There's almost no residue whilst carbon dioxide is used, however it's a fairly luxurious method of extraction.

Enfleurage

Long in the past, this approach emerge as used to seize the sensitive heady scent of orange blossoms, jasmine, and one in all a type plant life thru manner of mixing it with animal fat. The fats and plant mixture is then pressed amongst plates of glass. After severa days, the flowers are modified with sparkling ones, and so the approach repeats until the fats is saturated with the desired plant aromatics. Apart from hobbyists, this approach isn't appreciably used anymore.

Understanding Shelf Life

Essential oils are exceedingly touchy, that's why we use distinct extraction strategies. This makes the right storage of essential oils essential. After all, no person desires their luxurious neroli or agarwood essential oils going off! The shelf life, useful homes, and terrific of essential oil are appreciably depending on the garage technique (How to Store Essential Oils to Maximize Oil Life— Helpful Tips, 2019). When saved nicely, crucial oils can nicely final for as much as a 365 days or longer.

Essential Oils Can Expire!

Essential oils do expire and may end up risky to apply. This makes the proper garage and managing of your vital oils essential to get the maximum out of the product. The incredible of vital oils starts offevolved to mention no the minute we crack open the seal of the bottle, exposing the contents to oxygen. Oxidation reasons important oils to lose their splendid aroma, as well as any nourishing advantages that may be present. Citrus critical oils are in particular touchy to oxidation, often expiring inner six months after being opened. Not all important oils expire on the identical rate though. Some woody- and earthy-smelling crucial oils (like patchouli, sandalwood, and ylang-ylang) take longer to lose their performance and grow to be smelling higher with maturity. So an critical oil's shelf life can range significantly, relying on the chemical additives inside.

Oils containing monoterpenes, which include citrus, Siberian fir, tea tree, and cypress oxidize the quickest, at the same time as oils with sesquiterpenes or sesquiterpenols very last a first rate deal longer (Williamson, 2017). Essential oils containing sesquiterpenes encompass cedarwood, patchouli, sandalwood, and vetiver. Worth considering is that vital oils used in creams, sprays, and lotions can be trouble to microbial boom, which shortens the shelf existence of those merchandise drastically.

How to Spot Expired Essential Oil

Other factors that affect an important oil's shelf existence encompass the fine of the plant substances used, the extraction technique used, and the garage and coping with of the product in the course of delivery. It's a sensitive product, and there are pretty a few variables that shorten the shelf lifestyles of essential oils. Knowing this, it's miles critical that we apprehend how to tell if our oil has prolonged long gone lousy. The 4 hints beneath will assist you come to be aware about an expired essential oil without fail.

Take Note of the Aroma

Some oils lose their aroma, at the identical time as others adopt a stronger and ugly scent. Oils immoderate in limonene (citrus critical oils) often scent lousy while expired.

Look for Changes in Color

Essential oils frequently trade colour as they attain the cause their shelf lifestyles, for example

• Yarrow (Achillea millefolium) can flip from blue to brown (How to Avoid the Dangers of Expired Oils, 2018).

• Peppermint (Mentha x piperita) will undertake a greenish shade over time.

Most important oils are a clean liquid, with rarely any oily feeling to them. Some oils crafted from blue tansy, orange, patchouli, and lemongrass may be pretty colourful although! These oils are amber, inexperienced, dark blue, or yellow in shade truly, so hold a close to eye on any colour changes.

Spot Changes in Clarity and Consistency

If oil seems foggy or murky, then opportunities are it has expired. Citrus critical oils are an exceptional example proper here as they generally have a tendency to come to be cloudy with oxidation. Very antique oils commonly generally tend to alternate in consistency, becoming thicker and in addition viscous.

Follow those pointers and also you'll be able to spot an expired vital oil speedy! The shelf existence of critical oil is a sensitive factor; that is why all oils should be saved and dealt with as it must be. Expired crucial oils ought to not be used as they may be capable of cause infection, rashes, and unique unpleasant factor consequences. Lavender (Lavandula angustifolia) is one famous example that triggers inflammation whilst expired.

Storage Timeline

Proper garage and handling can make bigger the shelf lifestyles of your critical oils drastically. The table underneath shows how prolonged certain oils can be saved earlier than they need to get replaced. Keep a close to eye at the color, fragrance, and viscosity of crucial oils during the garage duration. In case you were thinking, it's miles possible to shop crucial oils within the refrigerator to prolong their shelf existence. Storing them within the refrigerator can display very useful for folks who rent essential oils handiest from time to time.

After analyzing this ebook, you'll be well-versed inside the powers and benefits of vital oils. You may additionally have a few vital oils in your private home proper now, or you may plan to buy a few speedy, so that you'll need to study out for expiration. I've made a smooth chart in case you need to check to preserve your oils from expiring.

Storage Period   Essential Oils

6–three hundred and sixty five days   Lemon, lime, bergamot, grapefruit, neroli, and orange oils

12–36 months   Angelica root, cypress, eucalyptus, Frankincense, juniper berry, laurel leaf, lemongrass, spruce, pine, rosemary, tea tree, and Siberian fir

24–seventy two months   Basil, clary sage, geranium, lavender, mugwort, cedar leaf, palmarosa, sage, peppermint, rosewood, and thyme

36–eighty 4 months   Birch, clove bud, jasmine absolute, Helichrysum, Roman chamomile, and wintergreen

forty eight–100 and eighty months   Black pepper, cedarwood, German chamomile, ginger, patchouli, myrrh, spikenard, sandalwood, vetiver, and ylang-ylang

Freezing Essential Oils and Extending Shelf Life

There are some locations wherein we should in no manner keep critical oils. Bright, humid, and warmth regions have to no longer be used for storage as they'll destroy the vital oils as an opportunity speedy. These areas embody window sills, bathrooms, or any storage space near a warmth deliver. Essential oils want to be saved in an area this is dry, faraway from direct slight exposure, and has a surprisingly regular room temperature; inside the ones situations, the beneficial homes of essential oils are preserved for longer. This may be a dry, dark, and funky cabinet, cloth cupboard, or drawer. But there may be one trick you can try and squeeze greater shelf life out of that bottle of critical oil.

You is probably surprised to discover that critical oils may be as it should be saved within the freezer! Sometimes crystals will shape, or the important oil can also emerge as foggy, but there's no need for alarm even as freezing. Simply permit the oil return to room temperature in advance than use. The time it takes for an essential oil to "thaw" can variety from a couple of minutes to a few hours, counting on the oil. To boost up the approach, soak the oils you need to thaw in a heat water bathtub. Ensure the bottle cap is saved on loosely; in any other case, useful volatile additives also can break out. Essential oils can be refrozen after use.

While the freezer can help to increase the shelf life of many crucial oils, it is despite the fact that suggested to hold a close to eye on heady scent, readability, and the viscosity of the liquid in its thawed u . S . A .. Other tips to growth shelf life embody

Following the producer's managing and storage instructions

Storing vital oils in amber-colored bottles, away from direct sunlight

Filling the headspace in a bottle with nitrogen can help put off the oxidation way. Nitrogen is used due to the truth it's miles heavier than oxygen and does now not react with the unstable compounds found in important oils.

Note the date on which the vital oil became offered; if it is listed inside the Storage Timeline above, you'll be able to determine how lengthy the oil can be appropriately saved.

Never hold undiluted vital oils in a dropper bottle. There is a hazard that the rubber of the dropper bottle can grow to be gummy and smash the oil.

Screw bottle caps on tightly.

Transfer vital oils into smaller bottles while the bottle turns into too roomy. Try to keep essential oil bottles as complete as possible; this minimizes the empty headspace within the bottle, slowing down oxidation.

Avoid placing objects into the important oil bottle.

Do now not preserve crucial oils or products containing vital oils in plastic containers. The crucial oils might also moreover react with the chemical materials determined in plastic, spoiling the oil/product.

Aluminum bins can be used to keep essential oils but excellent if the field is covered with food-grade epoxy. Aluminum boxes are beneficial for quick-time period garage and may be used to transport important oils. In maximum times although, a carrying case may be sufficient if we want to take our oils with us on a adventure. Just ensure that your oils are in amber-coloured glass bottles within the case.

The Power of Essential Oils

There's a chunk greater to critical oils than a outstanding scent! These oils have the energy to reinforce temper and promote relaxation; all of it relies upon on how they are used.

One of the most commonplace uses of vital oils is aromatherapy, a complementary remedy that makes use of one-of-a-type smells to beautify well-being. Studies have placed that those oils can be used to

decorate sleep.

reduce ache and infection.

improve sleep and decrease anxiety.

kill positive micro organism, viruses, and funguses.

relieves headaches.

Anecdotal proof moreover suggests that vital oils may be used to decorate the general situation of pores and pores and skin and hair as properly. The advantages of important oils are tied to the kind of oil. Below, we'll take a more in-depth look at a handful of famous critical oils and how they may be capable of benefit us.

Lavender

This oil is used to combat strain and pain and sell higher sleep. Its antiseptic and anti-inflammatory houses make lavender oil a popular issue in skin care regimens.

The super lavender critical oil will scent woody and earthy. Lower-exceptional lavender oils commonly have a sweet perfume. Lavender is a moderate important oil that is extensively used to sell rest. My preferred way to apply lavender oils is to feature some drops to my tub after a tough day or combine it with a base oil to create a pores and pores and skin-loving rubdown oil.

It should be said that lavender oil must now not be used on younger boys as it has the ability to disrupt their hormones. Research decided that every lavender and tea tree oil have estrogen-like homes, that may impact puberty and boom (Endocrine Society, 2018).

Tea Tree

Tea tree oil is pretty robust and is popularly used as an antiseptic, antimicrobial, or antifungal. This oil is frequently used inside the conflict towards zits, ringworm, and Athlete's foot. Tea timber need to be diluted in advance than use, but we are capable of make an exception while treating pimples. Simply dab some tea tree oil onto a cotton swab and follow it right now to the pimples; this will help clear up acne faster. Be cautious now not to overdo it, as tea tree can aggravate and burn the pores and skin at the same time as carried out in more.

For the remedy of athlete's foot and ringworm, the oil is diluted with carrier oil after which applied to the affected regions. Tea tree oil need to in no manner be applied in a diffuser if small kids and animals are around, because the oil can be neurotoxic. Early in my vital oil journey, I followed internet advice which claimed that tea tree oil is specifically effective at softening stubborn ear wax. Placing the oil in my ear canal come to be pretty a terrible concept as I'd later find out. The tea tree dried out my ear canal, leaving it angry and infected. I nonetheless needed to cope with stubborn ear wax on pinnacle of it all.

Frankincense

Called the "king of oils," Frankincense is idea to assist decorate temper, assist with contamination, and promotes sleep. Research positioned that the oil may be beneficial for allergies sufferers and can even prevent gum disorder (Health Benefits of Frankincense Essential Oil, n.D.). The oil has a extraordinarily spiced, woody perfume and is frequently implemented in aromatherapy and pores and skin lotions.

Peppermint

This oil is a cited anti-inflammatory, antifungal, and antimicrobial. It can be used to ease complications, enhance mood, and may combat fatigue. The oil has a cooling impact at the identical time as completed topically, making it very powerful at bringing consolation to a dry and itchy scalp. Due to the oil's antimicrobial and anti inflammatory residences, it could be used alternatively for tea tree to cope with acne.

One of my favored techniques to use peppermint oil is to mix a few drops into a few provider oil. From there, I'll observe a tiny amount beneath my nose and a few to my temples. It in no manner fails to open a stuffy nose and might help to relieve a sinus headache in the technique.

Eucalyptus

Eucalyptus is a extremely good critical oil to have handy at the same time as flu season begins offevolved! This oil soothes a stuffy nostril and opens nasal passages, but it is able to moreover eliminate bloodless sores and pain. When the use of eucalyptus oil, generally dilute it with a carrier oil earlier than software program. Be careful with oil round youngsters and pets as it is able to have risky factor consequences. For short remedy from bloodless sores, I observe a drop of eucalyptus oil neat to the cold sore as soon as an afternoon. After a few days, the cold sore vanishes with out a hint. This software method isn't always with out hazard as I've burned my pores and skin from time to time at the same time as the use of an excessive amount of of a specific oil.

Lemon

Extracted from lemon peels, this oil is normally diffused or implemented topically. The oil is idea to lessen pain, soothe nausea, ease tension, and produce consolation to mild melancholy signs and symptoms and signs and signs and symptoms. Lemon oil is likewise antibacterial and might assist to decorate the cognitive characteristic of Alzheimer's patients (Liu et al., 2020). I love diffusing lemon to offer me a touch mood enhance late morning or early afternoon even as my electricity ranges taper off.

The oil is typically strong to apply for aromatherapy and topical applications. When used topically, it need to be noted that lemon oil might also moreover make the pores and pores and skin extra sensitive to daylight hours, therefore developing the threat of sunburn. It is suggested to avoid direct sun publicity after the use of lemon important oil. The identical holds actual for grapefruit, orange, bergamot, lime, and lemongrass critical oils.

Rosemary

Rosemary critical oil is pretty flexible! It repels pleasant bugs, boosts temper, and might cope with hair loss. Studies located that rosemary oil is as powerful as minoxidil to address male pattern baldness (McCulloch, 2018). During the have a examine, people with male pattern baldness were asked to rubdown their scalps with diluted rosemary essential oil. The oil turned into finished times each day for six months, and the consequences had been in evaluation to people the usage of minoxidil. The findings indicated that the participants who used rosemary oil professional a comparable growth in hair thickness to folks who used minoxidil. Other studies indicates that rosemary oil can be beneficial to fight patchy hair loss as properly.

If you're looking for to deliver your locks a lift, attempt mixing a few drops of rosemary oil into your favored conditioner! The oil is commonly secure to apply in aromatherapy and in topical programs; but, if you are pregnant or be concerned via excessive blood stress or epilepsy, it is first rate to avoid the usage of rosemary essential oil genuinely.

Using Essential Oils Correctly

Essential oils are quite centered and need to be diluted in advance than use. To offer you with an idea of the manner targeted those oils are, keep in mind this for a 2d. If we favored to make one pound of peppermint important oil, we'd need 250 kilos of mint leaves! That's some of plant goodness focused in a single small bottle. When the usage of important oils, we only want some drops.

Try no longer to apply vital oils automatically as our our our bodies can come to be used to the oils, probably decreasing the effectiveness. It is a outstanding concept to offer your frame and senses a smash from important oils from time to time. This reduces the danger the oils can also additionally reason unsightly side outcomes (such as a rash or itching). With that being stated, allow's check the excellent techniques crucial oils are used.

Diffusing

Falling underneath the umbrella of aromatherapy, diffusing vital oils may be a high-quality manner to beautify mood or dispose of a stuffy nostril fast. Simply aggregate the oil and water regular together with your diffuser's guidelines. Other well-known aromatherapy strategies can be used as well. These strategies are dry evaporation and steam inhalation.

Dry Evaporation: Place some drops of the crucial oil on a cotton ball. Place the cotton ball in a place in which children and animals can't obtain it, and sincerely experience the exciting fragrance.

Steam Inhalation: Pour hot water proper right into a bowl and upload some drops of critical oil to the steaming water. Hover your head over the bowl and inhale deeply. Drape a towel over your head, creating a mini "steam room" as you inhale the fragrance. This approach is especially useful to relieve sinus congestion.

Direct Application

Essential oils are frequently applied in topical applications starting from hair growth additives and massive skin care to nail fungus infections. By making use of these oils to the pores and skin, they may be right away absorbed into the body. Apart from a handful of exceptions, we need to commonly dilute the critical oil with a provider oil in advance than use. Suitable carrier oils include jojoba, coconut, and avocado oils. For available application, don't forget putting the mixed oil in a small rollerball bottle.

Ingesting Oils

Essential oils have to in no way be ingested. That's due to the truth each drop of important oil carries big portions of plant cloth, making it masses much less complicated to trigger unsightly consequences. These oils also can burn the lining in the mouth. Some crucial oils can cause harm to the liver and fearful system while overused. An instance proper here can be tea tree and eucalyptus oil, which are appeared to purpose seizures (Essential Oils one hundred and one: Do They Work + How Do You Use Them, 2020).

Safety Tips

Let's be real for a 2d. Essential oils paintings first rate, however some make faux claims that are not showed thru technological understanding, so be cautious and research the oil and producer earlier than looking for. I've heard many crucial oil enthusiasts claiming that a aggregate of geranium and rose can remedy eczema or that essential oils can remedy dread ailments. These claims are absolutely not backed through technological understanding. In this e-book, we'll simplest cowl oils whose benefits are set up thru technological knowledge, so it is able to feature a available guide as you find out an interesting international of charming scents.

Scientific proof assisting aromatherapy use inside the remedy of Alzheimer's sickness, coronary heart sickness, and Parkinson's ailment is missing. However, aromatherapy can be doubtlessly used to treat many awesome situations including bronchial bronchial asthma, insomnia, fatigue, contamination, despair, menstrual issues, arthritis, menopause, alopecia, and peripheral neuropathy (Cronkleton, 2019).

It is usually recommended that you ought to use vital oils with caution if you have hay fever, epilepsy, allergic reactions, blood stress problems, eczema, and psoriasis. I'll share a few super useful protection tips under that may assist to lessen the threat of ugly reactions.

Only use notable, natural essential oils. This is crucial as we don't want any fillers or risky substances in the oil. Research the emblem and producer similarly to the terrific manipulate assessments that have been completed at the oil. Opt for natural each time feasible.

Don't use critical oils inside the ear canal, eyes, mucus membranes, or open wounds. These oils may be quite disturbing to those touchy areas. One time, I used clove crucial oil in a determined try and soothe my inflamed gums. What a mistake that turned into! The oil decided its way right into a small lessen in my mouth, and it stung badly. Yes, the clove ultimately numbed the ache for a couple of minutes however left an unsightly flavor in my mouth. To at the prevailing time, I can't stand the scent of clove critical oil as it normally rings a bell in my memory of the vile taste it left in my mouth.

Always wash your palms after the usage of crucial oils.

Discontinue the usage of crucial oil in case you enjoy pores and skin infection, stomach discomfort, or respiratory infection (Lane, 2022).

Always dilute important oils with a provider oil. Diluting crucial oil does now not weaken the performance of the critical oil, it sincerely permits us to securely use the oil. As an delivered bonus, important oils will be inclined to very last an entire lot longer while used diluted.

Do no longer ingest important oils, regardless of what the label says. There are too many variables at play that growth the hazard of an unfavorable response.

Some vital oils are phototoxic. Sun publicity should be prevented for 12 hours after the use of the ones oils. Examples of phototoxic critical oils encompass Angelica root, bergamot, cumin, and lemon.

Never use vital oils on or near infants and animals.

After studying this financial catastrophe, it have to turn out to be clean that essential oils are applied in loads of fascinating methods. These little bottles of focused plant goodness hold many benefits! To recap speedy, essential oils are

powerful temper boosters.

can be used to fight hair loss, Athlete's foot, insomnia, and one-of-a-kind conditions.

may be applied in numerous techniques (diffusing, mixed with a issuer oil, or steam inhalation).

have variable shelf-existence starting from six months to severa years, counting on the oil and storage situations.

Learning a manner to pick out and use exceptional crucial oils modified my lifestyles. Using extraordinary oils produces superior consequences, so maintain studying for tips at the manner to pick out advanced oils.

Chapter 16: Choosing And Using High-Quality Essential Oils

Not all essential oils are created identical. I had to have a look at this the tough way. My first challenge into critical oils have become a disastrous, rashy one. Like many novices, I've heard about the virtues of important oils and preferred to revel in their goodness firsthand. Lavender regarded like a sensible, secure choice. So I figured I'd pick up a small bottle of some thing essential oil brand come to be the cheapest at my nearby grocery save. At domestic, I cracked the seal, blended some of the cloyingly candy liquid with a service oil, and generously massaged my temples to alleviate a brewing headache. The lavender oil did now not carry treatment like I hoped it'd. Instead, it left me feeling nauseous and having to address a rash on my face! I, like many novices, made two critical mistakes.

An oil is an oil. I assumed all crucial oils are basically the identical and that producers are arbitrary innovations to inflate the charge of the product. So I surely determined on a few component became the most inexpensive without inspecting the exquisite first.

I used the oil incorrect, together with way too much essential oil to the provider oil. In my lack of knowledge, I ended up the usage of the oil of a plant that I have become allergic to as well. My health practitioner turn out to be now not glad and made fantastic I understood that if one is allergic to a sure plant, their essential oils cannot be used. Although my reaction modified into quite slight, using the oils of plants we're allergic to may be volatile!

Many beginners are often tricked into shopping for important oils which might be inferior, that may destroy the enjoy. By reading this monetary spoil, in an effort to now not be your case. We in brief touched on remarkable inside the preceding financial disaster, but here we'll offer an explanation for concretely a way to choose out and use relevant oil. True friends received't allow you to buy fake vital oils and neither can we!

How to Spot Real Essential Oils

Whether you use vital oils to help you discover balance in the route of meditation exercise or simply diffuse it for the stimulating fragrance, it's miles without a doubt well worth considering what's honestly in that bottle that's been hiding to your cabinet. Keep in thoughts that no longer all critical oils are created with the purpose of purity in mind. Essential oils have been used widely for decades, however this does not advise it's miles regulated by means of the use of authorities. The inevitable end result is that a number of the ones brown or blue bottles we see on maintain shelves (or online) contain synthetic fillers, perfume oils, and extenders to boom the producer's income margins.

When it entails actual crucial oil, the high-quality is relying on numerous topics, together with

Quality of the plant cloth used and whether or no longer pesticides, fertilizers, and distinctive chemicals had been used to cultivate the ones flora

How the plant cloth is processed to supply the oil. Some vital oils are intentionally diluted inside the path of the processing segment and may be tough to identify.

The packaging and handling of oils impact the tremendous, shelf existence, and purity of the oil. Quality oils are continuously in a darkish glass bottle this is tightly sealed.

Some critical oils rent cunning marketing and advertising practices, providing themselves as "restoration grade" oils. Don't be fooled through this! As of but, a grading machine for essential oils does now not exist (Burlinson, 2022). Some sellers may additionally declare otherwise, declaring that their oils are grades A, B, C, or therapeutic. If you observe any bottles marked like this inside the wild, bear in mind it is definitely a advertising gimmick.

Signs of a Quality Oil

The nose is aware of! Using our experience of perfume is one of the great and fastest methods to decide if an oil is a excessive outstanding or a knockoff. This can take time even though, specifically whilst we are not superb what to smell for. Taking an introductory aromatherapy path can in reality sharpen our sense of scent and shop our wallets from inferior products. Don't worry if an aromatherapy course is not at the cards, even the experts test those three matters to make certain high-quality:

The Bottle: Plastic and volatile chemical substances in crucial oils do no longer blend. Plastic is idea to leach chemical substances and can break the contents and have to be prevented. Quality suppliers will promote their important oils in tightly sealed darkish glass bottles. These bottles are commonly amber or dark blue in coloration to shield the sensitive contents from moderate. Usually, the bottle is pretty small and tightly sealed. Sometimes the bottle may be sealed with an eyedropper cap, but more regularly you'll discover an orifice reducer in the putting in place.

The Label: Labels ought to us of a the Latin and commonplace call of the plant and the additives that have been used. The label on a bottle of neroli, for example, should take a look at some thing like this: "Bitter Orange Tree (Citrus aurantium var. Amara). Steam distilled from natural bitter orange vegetation."

The label want to specify how the oil have turn out to be extracted and the way the plant material have emerge as grown (herbal, wild crafted, traditional). The label should also specify if the oil is one hundred% natural and need to listing the internet contents. Labels speakme of "essence oil" imply that the contents had been combined with one of a kind oils. Pure vital oils best have one component.

The Source: The label want to point out the united states of a of beginning or loads range that may be regarded as a lot as verify in which the product originates from. If buying critical oils on line, the website need to nation in which the oil originates from.

Signs of Fake Oils

Sometimes it's miles amazing easy to inform if that little bottle consists of snake oil. Other instances, greater clues are preferred. In addition to looking for signs and symptoms of a pleasing oil, look for the subsequent tells to keep away from searching for a fake.

"Fragrance" inside the Label: If you examine "fragrance" or "fragrance oil" on the label, kindly move returned the bottle to the shelf because it isn't an crucial oil.

Nonexistent Oil: Some vegetation are mistaken for use in crucial oil manufacturing. So if you see a bottle classified "violet important oil" or "inexperienced apple crucial oil," I'd hate to interrupt it to you, but it's not a real component. Violets are too sensitive to use in important oil manufacturing. Yes, violet leaves can be used to supply critical oil, but this oil is not accurate to apply in aromatherapy. "Green apple crucial oil" but is the crucial snake oil, being the made from a hyped-up weight-reduction plan fad.

Latin Name Absent: An absent Latin and common name is a awful sign. These oils are likely a mixture of artificial perfume oils. Even if the bottle includes herbal vital oil, as an instance, lavender, there is no telling what the contents certainly are if the Latin call is absent. Lavandula angustifolia is not like Lavandula latifolia, the previous being English lavender and the latter being broadleaved lavender.

Check the Price: In the sector of important oils, the fee isn't commonly right. Low fees are a few element to be cautious of however so are very immoderate costs. In the instances earlier than multilevel marketing located important oils, the fee changed into in particular practitioner driven. Nowadays, heavily produced oils from groups striving to set up a "brand" may be overpriced. At the identical time, those businesses aren't generally transparent approximately sourcing and sustainability efforts that play a function in the production of those oils. Keep in thoughts that expenses can and do variety from 12 months to yr due to some of reasons. Comparing charges from some companies must deliver us an exquisite concept of what a honest price for positive important oils must be.

Blending and Using Oils

Now that we've included the essential fundamentals of important oils, it is time to make your very own blends! As you benefit enjoy and self perception within the use of essential oils, revel in free to particular your self along with your very very personal unique blends. Whether you operate vital oils to unwind or to hold your pores and pores and skin dewy and sparkling, you already know your body first-class. It might also moreover furthermore take a few trial and errors, but this is all a part of the a laugh.

Essential oils may be blended with others, or they can be used in my view. Use those oils to create scented scrubs, perfumes, frame butter, cleaning soap, and plenty of one of a kind personal care gadgets. Mixing oils are amusing, allowing us to take pleasure in distinct scents. These oils can then be diluted with a service oil, alcohol, or dispersing agent, relying at the intended use. Don't worry, you'll locate many recipes in this e-book (and in financial disaster 8) in which essential oils are the superstar. Below, we'll take you step-by using the usage of-step through the way. Adhere to the ones steps, and also you'll speedy end up a masterful author of lovely restoration scents!

Step One: Choose Your Scent

Different scents are used for one-of-a-kind issues. Some scents supplement every unique properly, like geranium and rose. There are brilliant fragrance categories and smells interior a category will be predisposed to aggregate well together. We'll test those categories below. That being stated, scents from specific commands can be combined as nicely.

Citrus: Fresh, exquisite, and zesty, those scents have a refreshingly clean man or woman, making them terrific at a few degree in the present day summer time months. Examples right here include orange, lemon, bergamot, lime, and grapefruit.

Earthy and Woodsy: These rich, warmth scents carry a lovely grounding balance to an oil combination. Think of scents commonly applied in men's merchandise—the ones musky, earthy scents—and you are at the proper song. Examples proper here embody patchouli, pine, cedar, oakmoss, sandalwood, rosewood, juniper berry, and vetiver.

Floral: Oils on this elegance supply the fragrance of freshly lessen plants and regularly have a powdery test. That's because of the reality these oils are commonly crafted from the plants of a plant. So take into account plants even as making your mixture, and you could't go wrong! Examples right right here encompass chamomile, geranium, rose, lavender, ylang-ylang, carnation, blue tansy, neroli, helichrysum, and jasmine.

Herbal: Pungent with hundreds of fresh notes, those scents are glowing and complete of existence. They are often used to raise the mood or to deal with something unique. Examples right here encompass rosemary, basil, thyme, and marjoram.

Minty: Fresh scents with a chunk of a peppery man or woman and cooling green notes. These scents (peppermint specially) are used to reconstitute inexperienced and lavender notes in a mixture (Aromatic Herbs, n.D.). Examples right here embody peppermint, spearmint, sage, and wintergreen.

Spicy: These scents are first-rate defined as aromatic and invigorating and are utilized in lots of oil blends. Examples proper right here include cinnamon, black pepper, nutmeg, ginger, tea tree, anise, and clove.

Step Two: Choose Your Notes

Some scents vanish fast. Other scents can linger for hours. How extended a heady scent sticks round is predicated upon on whether or not or now not it is a pinnacle, center, or base be aware. "Notes" in perfumery and aromatherapy usually talk to the timeframe a fragrance lingers. A smooth test with cotton balls can assist to illustrate this point.

Place three cotton balls at the kitchen counter. On the primary cotton ball, location a drop of sandalwood. Drop a single drop of lavender on the second one. The 1/3 cotton ball need to get a drop of sweet orange. Take be aware of the depth of each scent. Straight out of the bottle, we're able to fragrance all 3 scents quite strongly. Leave the house for a couple of hours. When you return, be privy to the depth of the scents yet again. It is possibly that at this component the candy orange perfume has vanished, but the lavender and sandalwood cotton balls are nevertheless going sturdy. That's because of the reality the molecules within the candy orange oil are pretty small, evaporating speedy into the surroundings. Sweet orange, like many citrus oils, are a pinnacle look at. These are the scents that we scent first, however they vanish the quickest.

Fast beforehand a couple of hours and we'll check that the lavender is dropping its intensity, on the same time as the sandalwood however smells fantastic. This makes lavender a center or coronary coronary coronary heart be aware. Lavender has slightly large molecules than sweet orange; this is why the scent remains longer. A few hours later, the lavender perfume may be long past, however the sandalwood can potentially linger for days because of big, heavy molecules that do not with out problems evaporate. This makes sandalwood a base examine. Base notes are used to function richness and depth to a perfume. I use this cotton ball test every time I need to make an extended-lasting perfume, as it gives me a superb idea of the way lengthy advantageous oils will final.

Early in my adventure with vital oils, I began wearing them as a fragrance. I'd test with splendid scents, usually restricting my mixtures to as a minimum one or crucial oils diluted with a organisation. Sweet orange end up (and despite the fact that is) a favorite, however the delicious citrusy scent vanished in reality by using the use of lunchtime. With the lavender oil rash disaster despite the truth that smooth in my mind, I did no longer need to go through the day continuously reapplying the candy orange aggregate and threat a response. No, I changed into satisfied the logo of sweet orange I used end up inferior. So in my valiant try and find out a brand whose sweet orange lasted longer (and masses of cotton ball experiments later), I determined a totally crucial lesson: pinnacle notes will normally be the number one to move, no matter the hollow you burn to your price range.

If you want your mixture to maintain its aroma for longer, pick a amazing base look at (Hughes, 2022). Below, I'll share examples of oils that fall into every beauty.

Top Notes: Typically evaporates within hours. Anise, basil, bergamot, citronella, grapefruit, lemon, lemongrass, lime, peppermint, spearmint, and tangerine fall on this elegance.

Middle/Heart Notes: Usually lasts up to four hours. Allspice, cardamom, carrot seed, Roman and German chamomile, clary sage, cinnamon leaf, cypress, geranium, ginger, neroli, pine, rose and ylang-ylang are considered center notes.

Base Notes: Has the functionality to very last for days. Angelica root, balsam, clove, helichrysum, myrrh, Frankincense, oakmoss, and patchouli are famous base notes.

Step Three: Testing and Mixing the Blend

Now which you've decided on your scent and the notes, it's time to test the mix. For this step, you'll need a few cotton swabs. Take your chosen oils and drop a few critical oil at the swab. A single drop must be enough. Use a clean swab for every oil you would love to encompass in the combination. Hold those swabs an arm's duration faraway from your nostril, swirling them in small circles in the air. This will supply us an concept of what the fragrance combination smells like in advance than committing any important oils to a combination. Change the cotton swabs and oils until you discover a mixture this is appealing on your senses. Cotton balls can be used to test the fragrance in the equal manner.

Once you've pinned down the combo of scents which you like, mixture it following the 1-2-3 rule. That is, for every drop of the base note, upload drops of the middle look at and 3 of the pinnacle be conscious. I'd generally blend one drop of sandalwood, drops of lavender, and three drops of candy orange crucial oil to create a pleasant and lasting heady scent.

Always aggregate vital oils collectively first earlier than including a provider or diluting the oils. Use a pipette or dropper to drop correct quantities of your top, center, and base notes right into a easy (preferably glass) mixing bowl. Dilute the oils and transfer them to a darkish glass bottle for storage and use.

A Note on Diluting Oils

There are special strategies to dilute essential oils, relying in your intended cause. If you want to apply critical oils at the pores and skin, it's miles incredible to use a company oil. Carrier oils are commonly vegetable-based totally completely oils. If you've got got were given touchy and pimples-inclined pores and skin or are in fact unsure which provider oil to select out, try the use of jojoba oil. Jojoba oil is appropriate for all pores and skin kinds and mimics our pores and pores and skin's natural oils, making it an great preference to leave the pores and skin moisturized with out clogging (Gad et al., 2021). Other particular provider oils encompass avocado, almond, apricot seed, coconut, grape seed, hemp seed, and rosehip oil.

When we want to use vital oils in a chilled bathtub, it's remarkable to apply a dispersing agent. This helps the oil spread thru the bathtub thoroughly. While some provider oils may be used as a dispersing agent, they typically are too thick to use for this reason. Jojoba oil makes for an fantastic dispersing agent, as does candy almond oil. These oils are moderate with a liquid viscosity. Other dispersing entrepreneurs we will use are milk or honey.

Want a perfume? Mix your oils with a few alcohol. If you pick an oil-based totally actually perfume, use jojoba oil as an alternative.

Step Four: Completing the Blend

This is the very last step to completing an critical oil mixture. First, we'll need to determine the share of additives wanted. This will depend upon the way you recommend to apply your oil combo. The manual beneath can assist with that.

Purpose   Essential Oil Blend Dilution Ratio

Massage oil   15–20 drops to an ozof provider oil

Massage cream   15–20 drops to an ozof base cream

Lotions and pores and skin oils   three–15 drops to an oz.. Of provider oil

Baths   2–12 drops constant with ounce of dispersing agent

Compresses   3–4 drops to an ouncesof water

Ointments   12–30 drops in keeping with ounce of base ointment

Foot baths   Use four–6 drops in general for the footbath

Shampoo and conditioner   20–30 drops in line with cup of shampoo or conditioner

Perfume   10–15 drops in six oz.. Of alcohol or jojoba oil

The blending element is pretty easy as fast as we've decided dilution ratio. Simply combine all our materials in a tumbler bowl or bottle and use a spoon or wooden stir stick to combine. Always mix important oils first in advance than diluting. When the factors are thoroughly covered, transfer the combination into a glass vial or bottle for garage. Make positive to use an amber or darkish blue glass vessel to protect the touchy factors from light and save them in a fab, darkish region. Blended oils may be saved in the fridge.

Carrier oils do not final indefinitely. Blends containing sesame, rosehip, or sweet almond oil can be effectively stored for six months to a year. Jojoba and coconut oil are the exceptions and can final an entire lot longer as the ones oils are very strong.

Allow the oil mixture to mature for 3 days earlier than smelling it over again. Take test of any big changes inside the perfume. This will provide you with an fantastic clue about how the mix will age. By growing older some blends we're able to find out extra pleasurable scents. At this stage, your important oil mixture is now prepared to apply.

Choosing an Application Method

Scents can effect our emotions and cognition, making them useful to lessen the outcomes of strain (Kadohisa, 2013). So no matter how we pick out to apply and exercise crucial oils, so long as we are capable of odor them, they'll have the electricity to raise our moods and decrease strain. The desk underneath takes a better check the benefits and drawbacks of a number of the maximum famous techniques vital oils are carried out.

Application Method : Diffuser

Advantages : Disperses critical oils into the air, stimulating our experience of heady scent. Different forms of diffusers to choose from ceramic, electric, lamp earrings, candles, reed diffusers, and ultrasonic. Makes the room/domestic smell wonderful!

Disadvantages : Starting with diffusers and important oils may be high-priced. Can be intimidating expertise which oils to diffuse on the identical time as you are sound asleep, studying, or enjoyable.

Application Method : Dry Evaporation

Advantages : This technique is price range-high-quality and requires no particular device, high-quality cotton balls and essential oils! Useful for small areas, along aspect a car, air vent, closet, or pillowcase.

Disadvantages : Does not deliver the same perfume depth as a diffuser.

Application Method : Inhaling/Steam Inhalation

Advantages : The easiest technique is to in fact open a bottle of vital oil and take a deep sniff, however this technique is not encouraged. Steam inhalation is beneficial to clear sinuses and nice splendor remedies.

Disadvantages : The perfume is extremely centered in the bottle and may get worse touchy noses. The risk of undiluted critical oils touching your pores and pores and pores and skin exists with this approach. With steam inhalation, there may be a hazard of steam burns. The perfume may be overpowering and stressful if an excessive amount of vital oil is used for steam inhalation.

Application Method : Topical Applications

Advantages : Allow the goodness of vital oils to be absorbed right away through the pores and skin. Topical programs variety extensively from creams, oils, serums, and muscle rubs, making it clean to apply important oils for a specific motive (along side relieving muscle ache or as a fragrance).

Disadvantages : Can motive allergic or pores and pores and skin reactions. May probably burn the pores and skin if the oils aren't diluted properly.

After this financial wreck, you should experience a hint extra confident around important oils, specially almost about

spotting pleasant essential oils.

growing oil blends in order to stimulate your senses.

diluting oil blends as it should be.

Feeling prepared to test? In the following chapter, we'll take a deep dive into a global of suitable and uplifting scents that can combat anxiety. Keep reading to discover essential oils that can help to decorate our everyday lives.

Chapter 17: Best Essential Oils For Anxiety

Essential oils need to have a massive impact on our emotional well-being, a assertion that is backed through manner of technological information. A 2016 have a test investigated if the perfume of rose water had a measurable effect on tension stages. As you can guess, the results were pleasantly unexpected! The researchers said that rose water pretty reduced tension in the experiment individuals, enhancing their emotional situation (Barati et al., 2016). That is best one in all many advantages we will revel in from nature's pharmacy.

That being stated, essential oils shouldn't be dealt with as a miracle remedy for emotional troubles. When used as a supplement to appropriate health facility treatment, powerful important oils have the functionality to help our emotional nicely being (Lauron, 2021). It is the ones oils that we'll be taking a better have a check on this monetary wreck. Bear in thoughts that we're anybody. What may match properly for me may not be as effective for every different. Part of the fun is experimenting and finding the oils and combos that do the trick for you. My pal loved to use lavender to appease her nerves, whereas I decided bergamot to be greater powerful for me. Essential oils can be a chunk of a self-discovery device. I apprehend I'm continuously keen to check inside the hopes to discover new favorites. I'm confident you'll find out new favorites too!

Essential oils are crafted from aromatic molecules. These molecules are unstable (evaporate fast). What makes these molecules particular is their functionality to stimulate the thoughts even as inhaled, providing triggers, which have the capacity to have an effect on our feelings (Fung et al., 2021). Below, I've assembled a listing of vital oils which can be notably used to assuage anxiety. You'll be added to every oil, empowering you to use them with a bit of good fortune by the time you reach the prevent of the financial ruin.

Bergamot: Awesome in the Diffuser

Bergamot has a great and uplifting citrus aroma and is made from the peel of the Citrus bergamia fruit. A 2017 check located that bergamot crucial oil can enhance fantastic emotions at the same time as inhaled for at least 15 minutes (Han et al., 2017). It is strongly believed that this oil may additionally assist to lessen pressure.

What It Smells Like: A complicated citrussy, candy-however-tart perfume. The perfume is quite smooth and is similar to lime with herbal and floral undertones.

What It's Good For: The oil is usually utilized in aromatherapy to appease tension and stress. Inhaling the oil is concept to beneficial useful useful resource digestion and metabolism (Bergamot Oil—Uses, Benefits and Recipes, n.D.). It makes a clean room spray and is beneficial to do away with odors. In beauty applications, bergamot can soothe cracked pores and pores and skin and heels and is often used to add more sheen to hair.

There are many other makes use of for bergamot, although. I've only listed some of the most common use instances proper right here.

Best Way to Use: Diffused or inhaled proper away. When utilized in a diffuser, use three to four drops. If you're the usage of the oil topically, dilute up to 2 drops with four ozof provider oil to use.

Combines Best With: Lavender, patchouli, or lime to create a relaxing and uplifting essential oil aggregate.

Warnings: This oil has photosensitive capabilities, because of this it will react to sun exposure, in all likelihood burning the skin. Perform a pores and pores and pores and skin check earlier than the use of Bergamot important oil.

Personal Take: I loved this vital oil from the begin. I favored to try a few issue aside from lavender and determined the sweet, citrusy fragrance attractive. The fragrance lingers however does not overpower, making it a super critical oil to apply in a diffuser. I love the use of bergamot critical oil in my shampoos and conditioners to present my tresses that extra-wholesome gleam.

Chamomile: For Better Sleep

Chamomile tea is widely known to have sedative consequences, and the essential oil isn't always any exception. The essential oil is backed via robust research, a 2016 have a have a look at mainly backs the oil's anxiety-decreasing power. Researchers located that the vital oil helped to reduce the signs and symptoms of mild to excessive generalized anxiety disorder (Keefe et al., 2016).

What It Smells Like: Roman chamomile essential oil has a candy fragrance full of straw and apples. German chamomile, alternatively, smells of heat, sweet herbs. Generally, Roman chamomile's apple-like heady scent is considered the exquisite.

What It's Good For: Chamomile can be used to ease eczema, relieve tension, soothe rashes, promote sleep, and assist in wound healing (Seladi-Schulman, 2019). It virtually is a numerous oil! Both Roman and German chamomile vital oils can be used for comparable functions.

Best Way to Use: Add as a good deal as seven drops to a diffuser to combat anxiety, the oil can be diffused 3 times a day (Nicholls, 2022). A deep sniff without delay from the important oil bottle can also assist to calm feelings of nausea. As a steam inhalation, use 6–8 drops of critical oil with a facial steamer or in a bowl of warm water. Inhale the fragrance for 5–10 mins. For topical programs, dilute 10 drops of vital oil in an oz.. Of company or base product.

Combines Best With: Roman chamomile pairs surprisingly with floral and citrus scents. Clary sage, ylang-ylang, patchouli, bergamot, and lavender all work well with Roman chamomile. German chamomile pairs well with most floral, citrus, and herbal scents, at the side of Frankincense or patchouli.

Warnings: Do not use Roman or German chamomile important oil if you are allergic to the plant life of basis. Please talk in your healthcare expert if you are using arthritis or blood-thinning treatment in advance than using the essential oil.

Personal Take: On days that I revel in wound up, I depend upon my Roman chamomile vital oil to unwind. The mild, amusing fragrance facilitates to take the brink off and maintains my hay fever in test! Diffusers with an automobile-off characteristic may be excellent useful, in particular at the same time as using critical oils at night.

Clary Sage: The Stress Buster

Clary sage is neighborhood to the Mediterranean basin. The crucial oil crafted from this herb can assist to relieve strain and tension via lowering cortisol stages and producing an antidepressant impact (Lee et al., 2014). This makes clary sages an extremely good preference to diffuse in a room for a chilled impact.

What It Smells Like: The crucial oil has an earthy and natural fragrance. It is similar to sage but softer and sweeter.

What It's Good For: Clary sage can provide our locks a healthy-searching look, promotes higher sleep, and can raise temper.

Best Way to Use: For a temper-boosting and energizing aroma that relaxes frame and mind, try diffusing the following critical oil mixture: two drops of clary sage, drops of grapefruit, and 4 drops of lime. For topical programs, use 3 to 5 drops of the essential oil to an oz of provider oil or base product.

Combines Best With: Pairs pleasantly with bergamot, chamomile, Frankincense, black pepper, cedarwood, lime, patchouli, rose, sandalwood, cardamom, or tea tree.

Warnings: If you have got got low blood stress, please speak it at the facet of your healthcare practitioner earlier than the usage of clary sage important oil.

Personal Take: When my head is entire and it's far hard to fall asleep, clary sage important oil entails my rescue. I place drops proper away on my pillow, and this lets in to calm racing thoughts, welcoming me to dreamland.

Jasmine: A Powerful Depression Buster

The crucial oil is derived from the flowers of the Jasminun officinale plant. Jasmine important oil has a effective effect on our brainwaves and terrible feelings with its calming and uplifting houses researchers placed (Jung et al., 2015). This makes jasmine a powerful fine pal in our aromatherapy toolkit close to improving mood. A staple in perfumes, scented soaps, and private care products, jasmine important oil is beneficial to hold round!

What It Smells Like: The rich floral fragrance of jasmine has a comparable bouquet to that of honeysuckle, but it is extra extreme with a musky side. The perfume is appreciably taken into consideration a universally attractive one.

What It's Good For: Jasmine is a well-known issue in aphrodisiac blends and may assist to alleviate pressure. The oil is a strong antioxidant (Wang et al., 2017), making it an incredible choice to use in anti-growing older and pores and skin-assisting serums, oils, and lotions.

Best Way to Use: Diffuse up to a few drops of jasmine essential oil for a mood-lifting aroma. Dilute four drops of jasmine in an ozof provider oil to create a sensual rubdown oil (perfect for those romantic moments). For topical packages, use 3 to five drops of jasmine important oil to an ozOf carrier oil or base product.

Combines Best With: Bergamot, clary sage, chamomile, lavender, geranium, neroli, peppermint, sandalwood, and rose pair particularly properly with jasmine.

Warnings: This critical oil can also additionally purpose an allergy. It is recommended to carry out a pores and skin patch check. Place a few diluted jasmine important oil at the interior of your elbow and look earlier to reactions over the subsequent couple of hours. If not something takes place, the oil may be used correctly. If a response takes place, it's far best to avoid the oil. Reactions to jasmine vital oil are uncommon, but they're able to appear.

Personal Take: I love the usage of jasmine important oil to create a sweet and extraordinarily spiced floral fragrance. Combine the subsequent essential oils: one drop of cinnamon, drops of vanilla, two drops of vetiver, three drops of jasmine, and three drops of orange. Blend with an oz. Of issuer oil and shop in a pitcher roll-on bottle. Makes a pleasing gift too!

Lavender: An Old Faithful for Relaxation

Lavender is virtually one of the first critical oils novices are delivered to. The oil is widely recognized to create a relaxing effect and might reduce stress. A 2013 test showed that using a 3% spray interest (18 drops of vital oil to an ouncesof issuer oil or base product) have grow to be sufficient to lessen the place of job strain of participating nurses (Chen et al., 2013). The oil has many programs and is extensively used to promote rest.

What It Smells Like: Lavender critical oil scents can vary significantly, counting on u . S . Of starting vicinity, manufacturing technique, and notable variables. Generally, vital oils made from Lavandula angustifolia or "actual lavender" have the maximum recognizable lavender scent and are usually utilized by aromatherapists.

What It's Good For: Essential oils made from Lavandula angustifolia are utilized in aromatherapy to create relaxing, soothing, and uplifting aromas. There are many cosmetic programs for the oil, and it's commonly utilized in pores and skin care, baths, hair care, massages, and personal care products. Topical packages are believed to help pores and skin rejuvenation, heal scars, and soothe insect bites and infection (Lavender one 0 one: A Helpful Guide to Buying Your Lavender Essential Oil, 2020).

Best Way to Use: Diffuse three drops of the vital oil to create a chilled environment. Up to 5 drops can be added to the tub to inspire complete-frame rest. For topical applications, dilute up to 6 drops of the critical oil in a base product or company oil.

Combines Best With: Bergamot, clary sage, chamomile, geranium, lemon, patchouli, peppermint, pine, rosemary, candy orange, tea tree, and grapefruit pair well with lavender.

Warnings: If you're allergic to the plant of beginning location, the crucial oil need to now not be used.

Personal Take: Lavender is a staple in my medication cabinet; it offers brief remedy to insect bites! I commonly practice one drop of the oil neat onto the chunk. Don't fear, lavender important oil is one of the few we will use neat on the pores and pores and skin, but it is usually a splendid exercise to dilute essential oils first.

Lemon: Sunshine in a Bottle

Extracted from the leaves of the lemon plant, the critical oil is a herbal mood booster with a sparkly tension-decreasing aroma. Research located that lemon important oil can be helpful to enhance hobby, concentration, and intellectual usual performance while studying (Akpinar, 2005).

What It Smells Like: Similar to sparkling lemon rinds. The heady scent is extra focused and smells smooth and easy.

What It's Good For: Lemon important oil is an extraordinary degreaser and is used in lots of cleaning products. In splendor programs, the oil is thought to exfoliate the pores and pores and skin and deliver the complexion a healthy glow. It is a very flexible oil this is used significantly within the aromatherapy and private care place.

Best Way to Use: To do away with sticky residue from bottles and surfaces, consider adding a few drops of lemon important oil to a rag to help with the cleanup. To diffuse and purify the air in a room, try the following important oil combination: drops of lemon, one drop of lavender, a drop of rosemary, and one drop of lime. To make an exfoliating scrub, add 4 drops of the important to 3 oats and water (Lemon Oil Uses and Benefits, n.D.). Up to 12 drops of essential oil may be brought to an ounce of provider oil or base product almost approximately topical programs.

Combines Best With: Citrus oils, which includes bergamot, grapefruit or lime, combo pleasantly with lemon essential oil, enhancing the extreme and energizing homes of the aroma. The oil complements wintergreen, cinnamon, wild orange, and Douglas Fir properly.

Warnings: The crucial oil is phototoxic; therefore, we ought to avoid publicity to daytime, tanning beds, and UV rays for 12 hours after topical use.

Personal Take: Lemon essential oil is my thriller weapon to maintain silverware free from tarnish. It can correctly treatment the early ranges of tarnish. Simply add some drops of the oil to a cotton ball and rub the tarnish away.

Orange: For Clarity and Focus

This critical oil creates a relaxing nation and allows to maintain anxiety in take a look at, specially in pressure-inducing situations (Goes et al., 2012). The heady scent is vibrant and encourages a state of "relaxed alertness," it is first-rate for meditation.

What It Smells Like: Similar to that of smooth orange peels however more focused and sweeter.

What It's Good For: The shiny citrusy aroma allows to easy the thoughts and can remove undesirable odors at the same time as subtle (Orange Essential Oil, n.D.). In topical packages, the oil might also help to improve the arrival of blemishes.

Best Way to Use: Diffuse five drops inside the morning or noon, for a calming and energizing aroma. Pair with lime, lemon, or tangerine vital oils to recreate a warmth-weather perfume, or combination with cinnamon bark and clove for a festive tour vibe. For topical programs, dilute as much as five drops per ounce of service oil or base product. Dilute 10 drops of orange critical oil with distilled water and pour into a pitcher spray bottle. This mixture is reachable for retaining linens, sheets, and towels smelling awesome.

Combines Best With: Basil, bergamot, cinnamon, clove bud, geranium, ginger, lavender, lemon, myrrh, neroli, nutmeg, rose, sandalwood, and ylang-ylang make awesome perfume mixtures with orange crucial oil.

Warnings: The essential oil is phototoxic; consequently, we need to avoid exposure to daylight hours, tanning beds, and UV rays for 12 hours after topical use.

Personal Take: On days when I want to live calm and focused, which incorporates running to fulfill a cut-off date, the fragrance of orange essential oil maintains me going!

Rose: The Ultimate Relaxation Oil

Gently steam distilled from rose blooms, the essential oil is thought for its fabulously rich and intoxicating aroma. The oil has powerful pressure-reducing houses and may decrease systolic blood pressure whilst used topically (Hongratanaworakit, 2009). The important oil encourages feelings of relaxation and is used in plenty of cosmetic, topical, and aromatic programs.

What It Smells Like: Characterized via a deeply floral and wealthy smell with notes of honey. The fragrance is warmness and wealthy with out being cloying.

What It's Good For: The essential oil is applied in blends that motive to reduce stress, relieve depression, and ache and boom libido (Stanborough, 2019). The oil is a staple in fragrances and splendor programs.

Best Way to Use: Dilute a maximum of three drops of rose important oil in an oz. Of carrier oil for a deeply exciting rub down oil. Diffuse two drops of the oil to create a warmth and fun environment. For topical applications, dilute up to 3 drops of rose vital oil in line with ounce of carrier oil or base product.

Combines Best With: Rose complements clary sage, sandalwood, geranium, Frankincense, ylang-ylang, and patchouli most pleasantly!

Warnings: It is normally advocated to perform a skin patch check in advance than the use of the crucial oil in blends supposed for topical use.

Personal Take: This strain-reducing essential oil combo is happiness in a bottle! Blend the subsequent for your glass roller bottle: four drops of rose essential oil, drops of patchouli, and drops of sandalwood in an ozof issuer oil.

Store in a roller bottle for easy software. Whenever you need a chilled floral pick out out-me-up, roll some for your wrists and inhale deeply.

Sandalwood: The Anxiety Reliever

Sandalwood important oil is made from the timber of the East Indian sandalwood tree. The roots are used as nicely. The scent is earthy and warm with anxiety-reducing traits consistent with a small look at (Kyle, 2006). The oil is normally subtle, inhaled, or carried out topically.

What It Smells Like: The crucial oil has a deep woody fragrance and is a popular base notice in many perfumes and colognes. The fragrance is corresponding to patchouli.

What It's Good For: Used to decorate sleep excellent, promote calmness, and enhance temper (Schaefer, 2014).

Best Way to Use: For a brief de-pressure, test drops of sandalwood critical oil to the wrists and inhale deeply. Use drops inside the diffuser or upload five drops to bath water for a deeply enjoyable give up to an prolonged day.

Combines Best With: The sweetness in sandalwood is going properly with lavender, geranium, and jasmine. The oil blends well with bergamot and grapefruit in case you are craving a candy, uplifting enjoy. For some component warmness and fantastically spiced, try blending the oil with Frankincense.

Warnings: It is outstanding to perform a pores and pores and pores and skin patch take a look at earlier than using the oil for topical programs. The oil should now not be ingested.

Personal take: One of my desired home duties hacks is this: upload 10–15 drops of sandalwood crucial oil to a load of laundry in the washing tool. It maintains the bathing device and laundry smelling easy for tons longer!

Ylang-Ylang: To Relax Without Drowsiness

The important oil from this yellow huge call-fashioned flower is a rest powerhouse. It is idea that the oil may also lower blood strain, generating a calming impact (Hongratanaworakit & Buchbauer, 2006). The candy floral heady scent is brilliant at the same time as we need to lighten up without drowsiness.

What It Smells Like: The fragrance is just like jasmine and is characterised through a heady, sweet perfume.

What It's Good For: Samoan islanders are maximum of the cultures who used ylang-ylang for rest capabilities. The oil can assist us to foster a terrific thoughts-set with the aid of lowering the signs of despair, anger, and low temper (Fragrance Facts: Uses and Benefits of Ylang Ylang, 2019). The critical oil is extensively implemented in beauty merchandise and perfumes.

Best Way to Use: For a deeply exciting rub down oil, integrate three drops of ylang-ylang with an oz.. Of carrier oil. Diffuse drops to create a relaxing surroundings or upload five drops to bath water for an intensely interesting second.

Combines Best With: Ylang-ylang typically works properly with many splendid oils, collectively with lavender, Frankincense, jasmine, bergamot, and rose important oils.

Warnings: Please perform a pores and skin patch check earlier than the usage of ylang-ylang in topical applications. Some humans might probably expand contact dermatitis whilst using ylang-ylang (Whelan, 2020).

Personal Take: Ylang-ylang is a staple in my perfumery toolkit! I love diffusing floral blends with ylang-ylang inside the path of the day to unwind.

There are many strategies we are able to use vital oils to relieve tension. From deeply fun massage oils to heavenly baths, there is a global of rest equipped to be observed. When deciding on essential oils for a specific cause, take a glance if any studies help their effectiveness. Always perform a pores and pores and skin patch take a look at in advance than attempting an vital oil for the primary time. When diffusing crucial oils, look at the ones protection hints:

Dilute essential oils following the proper tips.

Diffuse in a nicely-ventilated place.

Diffuse vital oils intermittently, commonly 30–60 minutes is enough.

This bankruptcy includes many essential oils with anxiety-reducing homes. Whether you're looking to

discover a natural way to decorate sleep outstanding.

maintain tension underneath wraps.

stability mood.

There is an vital oil that may help! If you're experiencing signs and symptoms and signs and symptoms related to tension, it is usually fantastic to talk to a healthcare professional.

Essential oils ought to have a effective impact on horrific emotions as nicely, however we'll take a higher look at that within the subsequent bankruptcy.

Chapter 18: Best Essential Oils For Happiness

At some component, lifestyles occurs, forcing us to go through conditions which can drain the happiness a ways from us. Just know-how there may be days like that is all the encouragement I need to search around nature's pharmacy for solutions. Fortunately, there are few situations that aromatherapy and meditation can't triumph over! I recognise vital oils came to my rescue at the same time as the global pandemic had most parents constrained to our homes. It turned into a disturbing and troubling time made greater tolerable with the help of essential oils.

There are many conditions in existence for you to impact our mood and normal properly-being. Whether you undergo the occasional bout of tension or low mood, there may be an critical oil (or aggregate) which could assist. I've prepare a list of vital oils that helped to hold the flame of happiness burning in my lifestyles. I'm remarkable the ones oils can do the identical for you!

Eucalyptus Essential Oil: Cooling and Uplifting

When you sense a bit low, the uplifting aroma of eucalyptus can be clearly what the medical clinical health practitioner ordered. Eucalyptus is nice diagnosed for its sparkling perfume and is substantially used to ease signs and signs and signs of pressure. Anecdotal proof elements to eucalyptus vital oil as a beneficial examine useful resource via waking up a sluggish thoughts.

What It Smells Like: Cool and smooth, eucalyptus vital oil is quite focused. A little goes an prolonged way.

What It's Good For: The vital oil is appreciably used to inspire mental readability. The oil might also moreover moreover have cleansing homes and is frequently included in cleansing merchandise. Diffusing or steam-inhaling eucalyptus essential oil may be beneficial to unblock stuffy noses as nicely.

Best Way to Use: Add 3 drops on your diffuser for fragrant use or dilute 5 drops of eucalyptus important oil in an ozof company oil for topical use. Place a drop or of the critical oil on cotton balls to deodorize rooms and small spaces.

Combines Best With: Cedarwood, chamomile, geranium, ginger, grapefruit, lemon, marjoram, peppermint, pine, thyme, and rosemary paintings well with eucalyptus.

Warnings: Some humans may also enjoy sensitivity, so it is recommended to perform a patch take a look at earlier than using the oil in topical programs.

Personal Take: When it's flu season, I regularly diffuse eucalyptus to ease a stuffy nose. The cooling impact is quite soothing.

Frankincense: For Spiritual Upliftment

The crucial oil is crafted from the aromatic resin of the Frankincense tree. The oil has a sweeter and more energizing fragrance than the resin, making it a famous preference for non secular, perfumery, and incensing programs.

What It Smells Like: The heady scent is a combination of earthy, woody, and balsamic notes with a hint of softness and splendor.

What It's Good For: Widely used and valued in aromatherapy and pores and pores and skin care applications, Frankincense is idea for having sturdy a laugh and restorative powers (Fragrance Facts: Uses and Benefits of Frankincense, 2016). Practitioners of African traditional remedy often chew Frankincense resin to beautify digestion and enhance pores and pores and skin fitness. In Ayurveda, Frankincense is valued for its capability to cope with arthritis.

Frankincense is frequently burned to purify the air.

Best Way to Use: For comfort from aches, combination 10 drops of Frankincense vital oil into oz.Of provider oil. Massage the oil into achy areas for fast comfort. For topical programs, dilute as lots as 5 drops of the important oil in an oz.Of provider oil. For use in diffusers, use one or drops.

Combines Best With: Lime, lemon, wild orange, cypress, lavender, geranium, rose, sandalwood, ylang-ylang, and clary sage combo tremendously with the candy, resin aroma of Frankincense.

Warnings: Before the use of Frankincense essential oil in blends for topical software, please perform a pores and pores and skin patch check. If any irritation or hypersensitive reaction is discovered, it's far counseled to avoid the use of the product.

Personal Take: On an emotional degree, I locate Frankincense to be very spiritually grounding and calming, making it pleasant to diffuse ultimately of yoga workout or meditation. The aroma is resinous with a candy and heat spiciness to it that stimulates the senses without leaving me drowsy.

Geranium: Convincing Rose Substitute

If you're a fan of rose crucial oil, preserve in mind adding geranium for your repertoire. In a pinch, this important oil makes a convincing and charge range-friendly alternative for rose essential oil even as we consciousness on fragrance on my own. The healing and emotional houses of geranium range from that of rose. The oil has a relaxing and balancing effect, which also can show useful to alleviate signs and signs and symptoms and signs of hysteria and depression. A phrase of caution: Using an excessive amount of Geranium important oil could have a stimulating impact on a few human beings. Use the oil gently until you end up used to it to save you this.

What It Smells Like: The oil has a wonderful and dominant rosy-floral fragrance that should be used sparingly in blends.

What It's Good For: Geranium essential oil has antiseptic houses, making it useful to deal with pimples breakouts, pores and pores and skin inflammation, and pores and skin infection whilst used topically (Orchard & van Vuuren, 2017). The anti-inflammatory nature of the oil makes it a sought-after element in lots of splendor products.

Best Way to Use: For topical use in adults, dilute 10–15 drops of the crucial oil with oz of corporation oil. For topical kids, a dilution of 3 drops in oz. Of provider oil is mostly a stable quantity to use. To beautify the pores and pores and skin-loving homes of geranium, do not forget the use of sesame oil because the carrier. The combination makes a available spot treatment and rubdown oil. Geranium is usually utilized in diffusers to heady scent massive rooms and spaces.

Combines Best With: Cedarwood, clary sage, grapefruit, lavender, wild orange, lime, rosemary, and bergamot make amazing fragrance combinations with geranium.

Warnings: Before the usage of geranium crucial oil blends for topical use, please do a patch check. If any infection or hypersensitive reaction occurs, refrain from the usage of the crucial oil. Reactions are unusual, but they could appear.

Personal Take: Geranium's candy dominating heady scent makes it excellent to use in a fave residence duties hack. For this hack, we'll make DIY potpourri. All you need to do is to accumulate your favored aromatic spices and drop drops of geranium important oil and your preferred important oils onto the spices. Present the potpourri in a decorative bowl to characteristic fragrance and flair to a room or stash it in a stocking to hold the wardrobe smelling awesome.

Grapefruit: Subtly Energizing

Many human beings don't care for this notoriously sour fruit, however the crucial oil is a very particular story! Cold pressed or steam distilled from the rinds of Citrus paradisi, we gain an oil that is a wonderfully uplifting citrus aroma. Grapefruit is splendidly energizing, making it an great desire to fight fatigue. When we want to lighten and sweeten an essential oil mixture, grapefruit is often a right desire.

What It Smells Like: The oil smells just like grapefruit rind, most effective extra centered. It has a exceptional tangy-however-candy citrus aroma.

What It's Good For: Research findings guide the usage of grapefruit crucial oil to balance temper, relieve strain, and in all likelihood reduce blood stress (Berkheiser, 2019). The oil has notable price in topical programs and may be used in the treatment of acne.

Best Way to Use: Dilute 12 drops of grapefruit vital oil to an ouncesof provider oil or base product for topical packages. For diffusers, add   drops to blends for an invigorating aroma.

Combines Best With: Grapefruit blends superbly with many oils, which consist of bergamot, lavender, ylang-ylang, rosemary, and one-of-a-type citrus oils. Try blending grapefruit with Frankincense for a lovable aroma. Grapefruit essential oil is available in sorts: crimson and white. Pink grapefruit important oil is the sweeter one of the .

Warnings: Please do a patch test in advance than using grapefruit important oil in topical programs. The oil is phototoxic, and publicity to daytime, tanning beds, and UV rays ought to be averted for 12 hours after topical use.

Personal Take: I want to diffuse grapefruit crucial oil within the morning, mainly once I enjoy groggy from a overdue night time time.

Neroli: For Emotional Well-Being

Sometimes referred to as "Orange Blossom Essential Oil," neroli is made with the aid of steam distilling the blossoms of Citrus aurantium. The oil is extensively utilized in skin care packages and may useful resource in emotional properly being. Neroli is concept to ease feelings of unhappiness and can be used to combat grief.

What It Smells Like: The heady scent is complex, intensely floral, and citrusy. The oil is exceedingly focused, so a touch goes an prolonged manner. Neroli's uniquely complicated aroma is often tremendous loved in low dilutions.

What It's Good For: The oil is broadly applied in aromatherapy and topical programs to fight despair, insomnia, surprise, and strain and guide mature pores and pores and skin (Neroli Essential Oil Uses and Benefits, n.D.).

Best Way to Use: Dilute a maximum of six drops of neroli crucial oil to an ounces. Of carrier oil for topical applications.

Combines Best With: Chamomile, clary sage, Frankincense, geranium, grapefruit, jasmine, lemon, rose, sandalwood, ylang-ylang, and juniper critical oils complement neroli pleasantly.

Warnings: Please do a patch test in advance than the usage of neroli for topical applications.

Personal Take: When I experience like pampering myself, this foot bath combination hits all the right notes, leaving my ft feeling cushty. Blend the subsequent important oils and add to your subsequent footbath for a piece of indulgence: four drops of neroli, 4 drops of Frankincense, 4 drops of fennel, and 3 drops of lemon. Blend proper into a slight provider oil (like jojoba) and add to a warmth footbath. Unwind and experience for so long as you choice.

Palo Santo: Clear Negative Energy

Native to South America, Palo Santo vital oil is taken into consideration a near cousin to Frankincense. They have a comparable perfume, and we use them for comparable abilties. For centuries, Palo Santo timber, resin, and oil have been used medicinally, specifically to address pain and pressure (Arakelyan, 2021). The oil is thought to smooth bad power and is believed to have a purifying effect on the thoughts and frame. Furthermore, the oil is a to be had mosquito repellant!

While using Palo Santo is gaining greater mainstream traction, it's miles important that we make sure we're shopping for vital oils which can be sustainably distilled from Bursera graveolens. Loosely translated, Palo Santo way "Holy Wood" and has been utilized by nearby shamans for religious capabilities.

What It Smells Like: The aroma is right, balsamic, and woody. The fragrance is super defined as a mixture of Frankincense, Atlas cedar, and sweetgrass.

What It's Good For: Palo Santo is quite prized for religious and medicinal applications. The critical oil is applied in vibration paintings to smooth bad energy, while clinical programs see Palo Santo is utilized in remedies for headaches, hypersensitive reactions, arthritis, anxiety, and depression (Palo Santo Essential Oil Uses and Benefits, n.D.).

Best Way to Use: Use four drops in the diffuser or dilute six drops in an ouncesof issuer oil for topical applications.

Combines Best With: Palo Santo must be applied in a well-ventilated place because it has a robust, dominating aroma. It blends with Frankincense, myrrh, citrus oils, lavender, and helichrysum.

Warnings: Please perform a patch take a look at earlier than the usage of Palo Santo for topical packages.

Personal Take: I discover Palo Santo very grounding and calming and frequently propose it to be used internal spiritual packages. The oil is in particular valued to smooth areas of terrible strength.

Vetiver: Emotional Recovery

The smoky and earthy fragrance of vetiver might help you revel in extra grounded while the scales of emotional balance and stress hints. The crucial oil is regularly used to calm tension and raise a lousy temper (Saiyudthong et al., 2015). So whether or now not or now not you are looking for a hint pick out out out-me-up or want assist falling asleep, opportunities are vetiver can help.

What It Smells Like: The important oil has a heavy, earthy aroma that is much like patchouli.

What It's Good For: The vital oil is physiologically grounding and calming, making it a sought-after oil while coping with pressure and getting better from marvel and emotional trauma (Vetiver Essential Oil, n.D.). In topical programs, the oil also can help to enhance the appearance of the pores and pores and skin.

Best Way to Use: Add five–10 drops of the essential oil to a heat bath to ease restlessness earlier than bedtime. Combine three drops of lavender and drops of vetiver and diffuse for a deeply fun aroma. It is pleasant to diffuse this mixture at night time time. For topical applications, dilute five drops of vetiver in an ounces. Of business enterprise oil or base product.

Combines Best With: Clary sage, ylang-ylang, and lavender make heavenly perfume combos with vetiver.

Warnings: Please perform a patch test in advance than the use of vetiver in topical packages, as a few people may also moreover enjoy sensitivity.

Personal Take: Vetiver and lavender is a sturdy combination at the same time as accomplished topically to the feet or the decrease lower back of the neck. I love the use of this aggregate to soothe a tired and troubled mind.

Happiness is only some drops of oil away! The vital oils blanketed in this financial disaster can be used on their non-public or in aggregate with one in every of a kind oils. At this point in our adventure thru nature's pharmacy, we've got that allows you to

pick out the best crucial oils to stability temper and fight strain.

diffuse energizing oils on the proper time of day (in the morning or afternoon).

hopefully mixture crucial oils for a harmonious fragrance.

A fragrance can do so a whole lot. It can growth the dark clouds of tension, or it can motive a exceptional memory. For me, it's the perfume of moist earth and straw that triggers fond memories of horseback using. Memory and the texture of scent are cautiously related, but we'll find out that link in the subsequent financial disaster as we search for crucial oils with reminiscence-boosting skills.

Chapter 19: Best Essential Oils For Memory And Concentration

Some days are mentally draining. On the ones days, I get distracted by way of way of the infinite procrastination opportunities on the Internet, not able to popularity however chugging endless cups of robust coffee. On the ones days, my mind have end up tired, fuzzy, and forgetful. Not the quality state of affairs at the same time as you want to complete pressing reports! Quite truely, I felt like I changed into going a piece bit off my rocker. Turns out, I had the conventional "mind fog" scenario. I'll make easy the time period a chunk later on this financial catastrophe. Sadly, many human beings bear in mind this usa of mind regular and undergo thru it each day. At the time as soon as I was experiencing it, I did not understand that a foggy mind is an indication that some self-care modified into urgently desired.

After some special morning of slaving through evaluations with an uncooperative thoughts, a reminiscence of my time in Italy surfaced. Nonna's recommendation now surfaced like a shiny beacon of desire, as I discarded the file and rummaged thru my table drawers attempting to find a small glass bottle. Taking a deep whiff of the fragrant aggregate, I felt the cloud of incomprehension growth its veil from my mind. "Rosemary clears the fog of a worn-out thoughts," Nonna advocated me prolonged ago. "Keep it close to at the same time as you figure or examine."

Nonna's recommendation modified the manner I approached paintings. In this financial damage, I'll percentage which important oils can help to preserve you at your pinnacle highbrow wellknown performance. These oils can be used in my view or mixed with others inside the e-book to create appealing aromas. Many crucial oils can assist with a foggy mind;

experiment a little and you'll find out a favorite very quickly.

Clarifying Brain Fog

"Brain fog" isn't a medical situation, it's miles a very worn-out thoughts—some factor that many people revel in. The signs and symptoms are pretty commonplace, as a 2013 test suggests. These symptoms and signs encompass being forgetful, trouble focusing, talking, and questioning, similarly to having a cloudy mind (Ross et al., 2013). Other conventional signs and signs include

An Inability to Focus: Focusing appears like an no longer viable task! In this usa, it is straightforward to grow to be distracted, and minor options frequently end up huge offers. Organizing your fuzzy thoughts can be pretty difficult. I apprehend I often flip to cat films and memes, making procrastination my new terrific buddy whilst the mind fog rolls in.

Becoming Very Forgetful: You might also additionally neglect about to run a easy errand or the paragraph you simply study. Your teach of concept is without problem out of region, and it is probably a undertaking to keep up with conversations. This is probably one of the scariest signs of thoughts fog. I perception I emerge as losing my mind even as it befell to me, which includes extra stress to my existence which worsened my forgetfulness. It's a vicious cycle: the more you pressure, the extra you forget.

Feeling Constantly Tired: A suitable night time time's relaxation is not enough to prevent tiredness. A tiredness that feels find out it impossible to resist seeps into your bones at times. No depend how masses caffeine or sugar you get to your gadget, the tiredness acquired't go away leaving you feeling irritable.

Spacing Out: Your mind might probable enjoy dull and gradual, and it's far difficult to encourage your self. When this takes region, my days normally have a propensity to bypass in a blur, and I find it very hard to do some thing.

If you are experiencing persistent fatigue, test-in together along side your healthcare expert. Many of the symptoms and signs cited above usually have a tendency to tie in with underlying problems, which incorporates an undiagnosed allergy, terrible weight loss plan, an excessive amount of strain, or bad drowsing styles (Essential Oils to Beat Brain Fog, 2021). Mental exhaustion have to be handled as a caution signal. I see it as my frame's way of showing me the "check engine" mild is on. The appropriate facts is that when you find out what's triggering your mind fog, it could be handled quite correctly. Even better information? There are important oils that can assist!

Black Pepper: For Alertness and Pain Reduction

Black pepper important oil does not contain piperine, regardless of what some belongings can also claim (Black Pepper Essential Oil Uses and Benefits, n.D.). Piperine is what offers black peppercorns that feature fantastically spiced bite. The important is typically steam distilled from the peppercorns of Piper nigrum and can assist to decorate thoughts fog with the useful resource of enhancing alertness.

What It Smells Like: Freshly floor peppercorns with a hint of floral sweetness.

What It's Good For: When applied topically, black pepper creates a warming sensation on the skin and is generally utilized in blends to address arthritis and muscle accidents. Simply dilute 3 drops of the oil with a provider and massage into the spots of trouble. Anecdotal proof touts black pepper as being pretty effective to reduce cigarette cravings when subtle. It might be worth a strive if you are seeking out to kick the dependancy.

Best Way to Use: To diffuse, use drops of black pepper critical oil. For topical programs, dilute a maximum of three drops in an oz. Of provider oil. Black pepper does its great paintings while combined with specific essential oils so don't hesitate to test.

Combines Best With: A harmonizing middle phrase, black pepper is frequently the bridge amongst pinnacle and base notes and complements the as an alternative spiced elements of a mixture. Combine it with bergamot, clary sage, Frankincense, lavender, clove, juniper berry, geranium, cedarwood, or sandalwood to indulge your senses.

Warnings: The critical oil can be very stimulating and use thereof need to be avoided in advance than bedtime. Please do a patch take a look at earlier than the use of the oil for topical packages. Black pepper essential oil in all fairness centered and can reason infection, so a chunk bit is going an extended way.

Personal Take: One of my creator pals swears via this: dilute three drops of black pepper oil in an ouncesof jojoba oil and rubdown into the wrists for remedy from pain. She suffers from carpal tunnel and often uses black pepper important oil, specifically on bloodless and moist days, to hold doing what she loves high-quality.

www.ingramcontent.com/pod-product-compliance
Lightning Source LLC
Chambersburg PA
CBHW051725020426
42333CB00014B/1151